River of Life

How to Live in the Flow

Marilyn J. Awtry

Marilyn J. Awtry

Shen-men Publishing
Sanford, FL
www.shenmenpublishing.com
December 31, 2010
Phone: 407-322-7585

ISBN 978-0-9830641-0-7
Library of Congress Control Number: 2007901877

Printed in the U.S.A.

<u>A Living Memorial</u>

to my
Mother & Father
Rev. William A. and Bertha E. Jackson
who established the foundation for my Spiritual Understanding

CONTENTS

PREFACE

WHAT ARE the Questions! Who has the Answers?

1. Do you feel life is just too tough?
2. Is everything becoming just another problem?
3. Are your plans not forthcoming?
4. Are things backfiring?
5. Does everything bad that could possibly happen, seem to happen to you?
6. Are you sick and tired of being sick and tired?

If you answered any of the above questions in the affirmative, it is clear you are doing what comes naturally just like most of the rest of us. Sadly to say, that is simply acting without thinking and realizing that the "cause" creates the "effect!" If your actions are not in accord with the Natural Laws of the universe, the results will be negative.

What is that you are saying? Natural Law? I never heard of it. I have heard of government laws, county laws, state laws, driving laws, divorce laws, all kind of laws—but Natural Law, never!

Now that we have discovered the real problem, let us try to assist you in finding a better way of life. It is to simply learn how to live in the flow.

INTRODUCTION

O NE DAY THE MAILMAN may drop off a letter or an email pops up on screen. The routine question appears — "Can you give me any information about Natural Law?" These requests stimulated a thought. Why not prepare a book of the compilation of the laws? Thoughts do create things.

Are you aware that you are the artist painting your picture of life? The brush creating the picture of your life is in your hand. You paint each and every stroke of that picture. Just one stroke of the brush could change your life. Have you got all the necessary tools? Your picture of life can be joyful, profitable, and secure. Or, it can be sad, costly, and insecure. Your picture is designed by the depth of your own under-standing of life. It is absolutely true that the action we take today creates our tomorrow.

Why not live a full and pleasurable life now? It is rather simple. Just seek to understand the spiritual and physical laws and their application in your daily life. It is a pathway that allows you to glide merrily along creating the life you desire. It also provides your soul to continue onward in its expansion into a higher consciousness.

"Every person has free choice. Free to obey or disobey the Natural Laws. Your choice determines the consequences. Nobody ever did or ever will escape the consequences of his choices."

ॐ Alfred A. Montapert, Motivational Speaker

After much research, my booklet *Natural Law Governs* became a starting point for this book. You are introduced to a detailed listing of both the spiritual and physical laws. The outline presented can be a baseline for the individual seeker of Truth. It can also be a tool for the teacher in a classroom setting. It is my hope that this expanded content will wind its way into the home as well as into the schools of learning. The information offered can help you establish a foundation to begin to go with the flow—live in tune with the natural laws. It can also lead you onward into a life-long search for more understanding of life here as well as hereafter.

Now is the time for you to stop making life difficult for yourself! Now is the moment to allow the Natural Law to be your guide! There is no amount of money that can buy that which living in accordance with the natural law offers you so freely.

Marilyn J. Awtry
December 2010

I.

NATURAL LAW

You the Co-Creator

YOU ARE A CO-CREATOR with the Infinite Source of the Universe. As soon as you have discovered the spiritual and the physical natural laws, you will find that you have opened your conscious awareness to a higher level of understanding. Once you begin to apply this knowledge, you will realize that you can create the pathway of life that you desire. This knowledge is incomplete without recognition of the divine spark that lies deeply imbedded within you. Yes, you are a co-creator with the universal power, the source of all. Remember that the importance is never in the challenges that come before you in life's journey. The importance is in the way in which you respond to each and every challenge.

We all came into the physical world with an attribute termed free will. We have the ability to think and to make decisions based on our thoughts and our understanding. We usually become acclimated to the physical laws in a natural way. For example, if we touch something that is hot, we will get burned. If we touch an electrical outlet, we will get shocked. We learn very quickly what we should do and what we should not do in order to assure our physical well-being.

Likewise, we have the responsibility of learning to live in accordance with the spiritual laws and protect our spiritual well-being.

Our every day experiences become our learning experiences. They bring about a greater awareness of the universal law as well as the man-made law. For example, if you exceed the speed limit or go through a red light, you will very quickly see or sense the motorcycle behind you with a big blinking-blue light. The tall stocky policeman on board responded very quickly to your error. Ignorance of the law, my friend, is no excuse! As you are ticketed, you sit fidgeting, you twitch, and you fret. Next, you become angry with the system. Then, you become angry with yourself. After all, you could have avoided the entire situation by just simply obeying the speed limit. You know that is the law of the highway and it cannot be ignored. Since your emotions are in high gear at this point, you do not accept the reality of the situation. You begin your pity party. "Why me, why me?" rumbles through your mind. "I always drive safely. I just make one mistake and I get caught." No matter what, you are required to pay the price for breaking the law. It does not take you very long to realize that for every cause there is an effect, and it is either positive or negative. In most instances, humankind has the mistaken idea that they can handle it all their own way. Well, it just doesn't always work that way. The man-made laws of the day prevail here and now, and the natural law prevails forever.

It is very similar with the Spiritual Natural Law. Spiritual law can simply be defined as a basic grouping of laws to live by. Most generally, people may become aware of the laws through their religious affiliations or in studies of awareness. Unlike the physical law, there is no physical traffic policeman to see that you obey the spiritual laws. That responsibility is left directly to you by that which is termed your conscience.

It is the nature of humankind to react to whatever the moment presents, in whatever way suits their fancy. Most often, we tend to act without first giving a thought to the reaction it will create. When we have become more spiritually oriented and function in a higher consciousness, we will also achieve growth in our soul—our very being. Then and only then, do we live our daily life in harmony with the spiritual natural laws. However, to live in this manner requires you to become spiritually knowledgeable. Biblically we are taught

> "Whatsoever things are true, whatsoever things are honest, whatsoever things are just, whatsoever things are pure, whatsoever things are lovely, whatsoever things are of good report; if there be any virtue, and if there be any praise, think on these things."

> ∾ Philippians 4:8 KJV

James Allen said "As a man thinketh in his heart, so is he." This thinking process is the umbrella of your life. It is your own shield and protector. Every single condition and circumstance is the resultant product of the thought upon which you acted or reacted. The power of your thought sets the energy pattern of either positive or negative into full swing in your life.

There is a quote that Zig Ziglar often emphasizes in his seminars that is very applicable to the natural law. He states, "He who chooses the beginning of a road, also chooses its outcome." Isn't that very true? The cause always brings about the effect.

If you have the proper thoughts and then apply them by making the right choices, you are able to create the life style that you really desire. At that point, you will find that thinking first does allow doing what comes naturally and that is basically meeting the requirement of the natural law.

Cicero said "Man was born for two things—thinking and acting." Tennyson said "Man is man, and master of his fate." If you take these teachings into consideration seriously, the floodgates of more spiritual knowledge will swing wide open. You will then learn that as co-creator you not only have responsibility for yourself but for the inhabitants of the universe collectively. You learn that we are all interconnected spiritually, even while we are abiding in the physical body. The famed English poet John Donne said, "No man is an island unto himself; every man is a part of the continent, a part of the main." This extends the importance of realizing your ability to create your every tomorrow. The knowing and practicing of the spiritual laws will, without a doubt, bring about a transformation in your life as well in the lives of those around you.

Carefully read the words of Hooker, as he reveals the reverence for the Law

> "Of Law there can be no less acknowledge that her seat is in the bosom of God, her voice her harmony of the world; all things do her homage, the very least as feeling her care; her power; both angels and men, and creatures of what condition sever, though each in different sort and manner, yet all with uniform consents admiring her as mother of their peace and joy."

II.

DEFINING NATURAL LAW

"The Natural Law is a process, not a power; it is a method of operation, not an operator. A Natural Law without God behind it, is no more than a glove without a hand in it."

ഔ Joseph Cook

I N EVERY AGE humankind has always respected the underlying control of the universe. However, the concept of that control, power, or force has been interpreted by various people in various ways.

Humankind has always recognized the existence of some kind of power. Yet, in its finite mind, it has never fully comprehended this invisible controlling factor. It has recognized that natural law is an eternal order of the universe. This is revealed in the changeless constitution demonstrated by nature.

Humankind has always recognized that it lives in a world of constant change. It has also comprehended that this world continues on with certain events following a pattern or a sequence of events (Law of Sequence, Law of Orderly Trend). For example, the sun always rises in the east at dawn and sets in the west in the evening. It never rises at noon or any other time during the twenty-four hour period. There is no question in anyone's mind when or where the sun will rise and set.

Humankind, in its state of evolutionary process, has further recognized there is an Infinite wholeness and none can be totally separated from the center of this source or power. Think again on the words of the famed English poet, Dr. John Donne expressed in *Devotions*

> "No man is an island entire of itself; every man is a piece of the Continent; a part of the main, if a clod be washed away by the Sea, Europe is the less, as well as if a promontory were, as well as if a manor of thy friends or of thine own were; any man's death diminishes me, because I am involved in Mankind; therefore never send to know for whom the bell tolls; it tolls for thee."

Humankind has always been inquisitive by nature. Today, we continue to seek an understanding of that power or source. Natural law affects everything in creation. Nothing, absolutely nothing, can stand apart from it. And just as no man is an island, so no man or anything ever created is free from the influence of the natural law.

In his book, *Ancient Mystery and Modern Revelation*, 1910, Wilberforce J. Colville lists the four aphorisms. They are:

1. "There is one law.
2. There is naught higher or elder than the one law.
3. The one law is absolute: beyond time, space and change, and transcending the principles of analysis, sequence, rhythm, balance, cyclicity and opposites.
4. The one law is the efficient reason of all things."

In *The Thunder of Silence*, 1961, Joel Goldsmith recorded that "God is the only law; a law which maintains and sustains the harmony and perfection of its own creation at all times." We, as a whole, recognize the universe is governed according to natural laws that cannot be set aside by or for the whim of any individual no matter what their status may be. Very often we read that the universe is governed **by** natural law. That is indeed an error. The correct expression is that the universe is governed **according** to natural law. It might be better understood by saying the universe is governed **depending** on the natural law.

There is absolutely no power that can enable anyone to escape the consequences of breaking the natural law. A very important point is the fact that the Infinite rules over both that which is material and spiritual. There is no division within the kingdom; the material and the physical are a part of indivisible life.

In *Life and Power*, 1902, W. J. Colville reminds us that "All things are governed by law has been the axiom upon which my mind has rested with a sense of entire security for many years. Outside of the law, there can be neither order nor justice...chaos would come again when the law ceased to govern. It is clear that the things of matter react on the things of spirit and the things of spirit react on the things of matter. We often hear the words, "as above, so below".

In *Swedenborg, Life & Teachings* by George Trobridge, 1905, quotes from Swedenborg's *Heaven and Hell are recorded as* "The natural world, and all it contains, exists and subsists upon the spiritual world, and both from the Divine."

These points are further amplified in *The Message of the Divine Iliad,* *1949,* by Walter Russell as he relates "For again I say, My One Law demandeth that man doeth My Will in all his creations by first giving the Light of his Self, so that the reflection of the Light returned to him in full measure, e'en as I give of My Light to My Universe and repeat the reflection of My Light forever and ever."

Since humankind is a part of nature, it can experience the fullness of life by living in proper attunement with the law. When we are in tune with the law, we are in tune with the Infinite. When we are in tune with the Infinite, all knowledge becomes a major component of our very being. Nature also clearly displays that it is in tune with the natural law. As springtime approaches plants sprout their greenery, buds form and soon are expressed as colorful scented flowers. We enjoy the beauty of the flowers, their color, shape, and their wonderful fragrance. Soon the flowers follow nature's path and the fragrance of the petals dissipates, the petals droop, and then fall to the earth from whence they came. The cycle is completed until springtime brings forth the renewal of life and another new cycle.

Having reached this point, let us review our question again; just what is this Natural Law? To develop an understandable definition, we will begin by utilizing, as our resource, *The American Heritage Dictionary, Third Edition*. From this source, we will clearly and rapidly establish a basis for the fundamental words connected with the term Natural Law.

Definitions

Law

"A rule of conduct or procedure established by custom, agreement or authority; a body of rules and principles governing the affairs applicable to a people; as a rule or principle of proper conduct sanctioned by man's conscious concepts of natural justice, or the will of a deity; a divinely appointed order or system."

Natural

"Present in or produced by nature; relating or concerning nature; conforming to the usual or ordinary course of nature; formed by nature without human intervention."

Natural Law

"A law or body of a law that derives from nature and is believed to be binding upon human action; apart from or in conjunction with laws established by human authority."

Nature

"Nature is best defined as the material world and its phenomena; the essential characteristics and qualities of a person or thing. In theology, it is humankind's natural state as distinguished from the state of grace."

As we continue, we find that terminology becomes an important factor in gaining the understanding of any subject. Very frequently, there is confusion because of the various terms used in relationship to natural law. There are bound to be many synonyms of the term natural law. These are words that can be used interchangeably.

The awareness that these words are synonyms can help us avoid unnecessary confusion. For clarity, alphabetically listed below are some of the terminology that is often used synonymously with the term Natural Law:

__Cosmic Consciousness__

__Cosmic Law__

__Divine Law__

__Divine Mind__

__God's Law__

__Great Spirit__

__Law of the Infinite__

__Law of Nature__

__Law of Spirit__

__Universal Consciousness__

__Universal Law__

__Universal Mind__

Our next step is to take all of the above terminology and bring it into a clear concept of our understanding (scientifically, philosophically and as it pertains to religion) and conclude how we will define natural law for this review. That definition is as follows:

"Natural Law is the law that a power or source (God, the Infinite) has set in motion to govern all that has been created or is in being. It is immutable and unchangeable and we know of no instance where the Source (God, the Infinite) has set aside the law in response to any human appeal, nor suspended that law for any other reason."

This conclusive definition of Natural Law reveals to us that our universe is one of order. We are not aware of any reason for that governing source to suddenly change its operation or the effect of it. It has been consistent and it will remain consistent. As mentioned previously, the sun rises in the east at dawn and sets in the west in the evening. The sun has never risen at any other time; of course not, for it is not in accordance with the natural law. Likewise, the light of the silvery moon brightens the sky at night. As a result of this orderly procedure, humankind accepts the fact that there is a definite principle or rule in control.

There are some individuals who term events or actions that are unfamiliar to humankind as miraculous or supernatural. It is a lack of understanding that tends to make one think erroneously. The term miracle or supernatural is a misnomer. Every single action that occurs in the universe is "natural and in accordance with the natural law." Humankind, thinking in regard to the term miracle, reasons that the law somehow has been suspended and now has become obedient to humankind's own command. At this point of our evolutionary process, we recognize there are many events that are not of our understanding; however, this in no way infers that the law has been changed, interrupted, or negated.

Natural law prevails! Life can never stand still. Change is the basis of nature. Let me repeat once again—there is a great deal of knowledge about the natural law that is beyond humankind's comprehension at this time. Without a doubt, there are many more natural laws that have not yet come into our awareness at this stage of our evolutionary process. Slowly, through time, humankind learns. As an example, we became aware of the Law of Gravity. Newton did not discover gravity. Rather, he came into a greater understanding of the laws of the universe and was able to detect and instruct humankind in how and why a forceful pull is exerted throughout the universe. Edison did not discover electricity. He did become aware of an understanding of how the currents operated and thus brought to us the wonderful workings of electricity.

Continuing with our exploration, remember that natural law is that law or set of laws that have been decreed from the beginning of time as a working or operational basis for all of creation. Without natural law, there would be no orderly occurrences or manifestations; chaos would be rampant. The natural law influences, defines, and controls all aspects of humankind's endeavors, not excluding science, philosophy, nor religion. These laws operate in every state of existence. They are established as universal in their scope and in their manner of operation. Natural Law is "a law unto itself." Natural Law expresses itself through many various changes in form. Nothing is ever destroyed nor lost in nature. Science has shown that nothing can come into existence by itself; there must be an initial cause. We understand that cause to be the Infinite Source, Spirit, or the common term, God.

Although natural law is often thought of as being very complex, it is basically extremely simple to understand. Natural law is the fundamental law of being, of having existence. Its purpose is to insure a progressive or successive cycle in the evolutionary process of the universe. Natural law establishes powers, functions, attributes, and phases through the various kingdoms or planes of the universe. It is these very aspects that cause one to seek the ideal of being known as self-preservation. The preservation of all life is the attainment of humankind's expression. Regardless of what obstacles humankind may try and put in place in an attempt to interrupt the laws operation, the law continues on in its successive pattern.

The laws listed herein include the material and spiritual aspects of life. There is no separation of the law no matter whether it pertains to science, philosophy or religion—physical or spiritual. It is all under one universal source—the Law of One.

III.

PHILOSOPHY OF NATURAL LAW

Wisdom of the Ages

T HE STUDY OF natural law has been expanded through time and more recently into space. In order to better understand the concepts of today, let us understand the foundation set forth by the study and knowledge of those who have gone before us; particularly, in the arenas of the sciences, philosophy, and spirituality.

In the early 1800s, Andrew Jackson Davis, the Poughkeepsie Seer, documented in the booklet *From Fire Mist-to-Man*, that "The laws that govern nature go on with a steady and unchangeable progression. They are not at any time retarded or accelerated and nothing can prevent the natural results of their operation. They are established by one great positive power and mind—and equally by a negative or ultimate equilibrium. Hence, their continued and united forces by the influence, which all things are actuated, governed, and developed, pass on in a steady process of progression."

Davis went on to express that "Every particle of matter possesses the same power which governs the whole universe and in which particles you see a representation and evidence of the Divine laws. For example, "In stone you see the property of the soil; in the soil, the property of the plant; in the plant the property of the animal or in animal you see man—and in man you cannot see, but you do feel the immortal principle."

In his writing entitled *Questions and Answers,* Davis stated "Men seek in vain and strive ineffectually with the ambitious logic to separate the Deity from the principles of nature. But we are more and more persuaded that the higher and grander the intellect, the less and less does it attempt to draw a line of distinction between the Laws of Nature and Nature's God."

In *The Debatable Land between This World and the Next,* 1871, Robert Dale Owen sheds further light on the subject. In reading his work, it becomes very obvious that the subject of natural law was a popular topic of the day. Owen states, "The idea of Natural Law, the universal reign of fixed order of things has been casting out the supernatural. The idea is a product of that immense development of physical sciences which is characteristic of our times. We cannot read a periodical or go to a lecture room without hearing it expressed." Owen continues by stating that "The Natural Laws are not only invariable but are continuous. They do not show themselves for fifty or one hundred years and thence cease to operate for a period of time. The action of Natural Law is perpetual from one generation to another generation—a direct continuity." He gives us further evidence of the law as he shares quotes of various eminent people of his time. These words of wisdom provide us with another step in the understanding of the natural laws.

The Bishop of Exeter at the University of Oxford stated "One idea is now emerging into supremacy in science; a supremacy which it never possessed before, and for which it still has to fight a battle; and, that is the idea of the law. The weather, thunder and lightening, crops of the earth, the progress of disease whether over a country or individual—the steady march of science has now reached a point where men are tempted or rather compelled, to jump at once to a universal conclusion, all analogy points one way, none another. And the student of science is learning to look upon fixed laws as a universal natural action of still higher laws belonging to a world whose phenomena are only half revealed to us."

In another firm statement, Baden Powell, a prominent man in physical science, stated "This modern turn of reasoning adopts the belief that a revelation is the most credible when it appeals least to violation of natural causes. Thus, if miracles were, in the estimation of a former age among the chief supporters of Christianity, they are at present among the main difficulties and hindrances to its acceptance."

A well-known representative of the Unitarian faith, Rev. James Freeman Clarke, stated "If I consider the wonderful works of Jesus as violations of the law, I should say they were essentially incredible."

In *Science and the Unseen,* 1883, Arthur Stanley Eddington explicitly recorded "The tendency today is not to reduce all to matter, but reducing it to the manifestation of the operation of Natural Law." He continues to explain "…that by natural law we mean laws of the type prevailing in geometry and mechanics are found to have this common characteristic that they are ultimately reduced to mathematical equations."

In *Natural Law in the Spirit World,* 1883, Henry Drummond, the philosopher, made it known that as he was commencing this work that "…a new word of the day was natural law." Interesting, isn't it?

As time changes, our vocabulary also changes and then, very often semantics seep in and cause additional confusion.

Drummond clearly points out that pursuit of the law became a passion of science as each new "so-called" discovery came about. For instance, it was felt that actual understanding or the discovering of gravitation was not as great a fact in itself, as was the "revelation" of the law expressed therein.

We quote Drummond as he simply expressed that "The fundamental conception of the Law is an ascertained working sequence or constant order among the phenomena of nature. Given this impression of law as order, it is important to receive it in its simplicity, for the idea is often corrupted by having attached to it erroneous views of cause and effect. In its true sense, Natural Law predicates nothing of causes. They are relative to man in his many limitations and represent to him the constant expression of what he may always expect to find in the world around him; however, that they have any casual connection with the things around them is not to be conceived. The Natural Law originates nothing, sustains nothing; the laws are merely responsible for the uniformity in sustaining what has been originated and what is being sustained. They are a mode of operation, therefore not the operators, processes, nor powers."

Drummond continually points out that when one studies and understands the Law, one stands face-to-face with Truth—solid and unchangeable. As an example, he says: "The law of nature is simply statements of orderly conditions of nature and what is found in nature. This idea is substantiated by a sufficient number of competent observers."

Drummond also emphasizes that "Natural Law is a great line running not only through the world as we know it, but throughout the universe; reducing it like parallels of latitude to an intelligent order. All of nature is in harmony; man in all his relations stands therein. As we study, we find that harmonious law is apparent in the physical, mental, and spiritual modes of existence."

He further clarifies his understanding by expressing that "The phenomena of the Spirit World are in analogy with the phenomena of the natural world requires no statement...the position we have been led to take is not that the Spirit Laws are analogous to the Natural Law, but that they are the same laws. The laws of the invisible are the same laws, projections of the natural not supernatural."

In *Ancient Mystery & Modern Revelation,* 1910, another of our great pioneers, Wilberforce J. Colville, has discussed natural law at great length. He builds all of his philosophy around the Law of Orderly Trend. This law states that "The law is under the operation of which order is universally made manifest from the grouping of atoms in formation of the minutest organism to the arrangement of the planetary bodies in the constitution of the gigantic solar system." In other words, the universe from the least to the greatest is governed in an orderly fashion.

Colville continues on by saying "That the law resulting of the many laws of the universe is really only One Law. The One Law is Absolute—beyond time, space and change. The One Law is sufficient reason for all things!" In his great depth of understanding, he expressed that: "No special event is divinely predetermined, foreordained or predestined. But, rather there is a sequence of Cause and Effect which no human power can vary." This theory also aligns with the Law of Continuity.

If we turn to Arcane Philosophy, the expressions for consideration are:

- ❖ Ex Nihilo nihil fit—"Out of nothing is nothing made."
- ❖ Ex Nihilo Omnis fit—"Out of nothing all things are formed."

Colville's explanation of these expressions is: "From out of nothing comes the cosmic substance from which all is made and to which all returns."

The three principles in all of Colville's thinking are:

- ❖ Substance
- ❖ Motion
- ❖ Consciousness.

He continues by saying that "We are living not in a dead but in a living world; not in an unconscious but in a conscious universe in which death is only a change of expression and birth an assumption of a new garment."

Colville points out "the paranormal operation of those higher or more recondite Laws of God, with which we are only imperfectly acquainted. We either call their effects miraculous or shut our eyes and deny they exist."

Concerning miracles, he states "So far from holding that which are called miracles are interruptions or violations of the course of nature and thus are regarded as Spiritual laws which in occasion action subdue, suspend, or neutralize the less powerful physical laws just as a strong chemical affinity subdues a weaker one but yet combinations strictly in accordance with the collective laws of the universe— understood or not understood by us at this time."

In *Science and a Future Life*, 1893, F. W. H. Myers presented that which he termed "Cosmic Law." Not only does he discuss rules which concern matter, motion, or abstract quantities, but principles which even if as yet but dimly understood, may conceivably be valid for the whole universe on all possible planes of being. Myers states "that the law is applicable to three principles: Uniformity, Conservation, and Evolution. All operations in the universe obey the unchanging law. This supports the understanding that all functions in the universe operate by immutable law. Further, we recognize matter and energy as indestructible. Finally, we believe all physical and vital operation in the universe follows certain obscurely indiscernible streams of tendency that the Source and God is not known." The three principles stated by Myers are

- ❖ "Principle One: Uniformity lies at the root of all Science.
- ❖ Principle Two: Conservation lies at the root of Physics.
- ❖ Principle Three: Evolution lies at the root of all Biology."

In his book, *In Tune with the Infinite*, 1897, Ralph Waldo Trine emphasized that "The great central fact of the universe is that Spirit of Infinite Life and Power is the source of all."

Trine continues on to describe the Spirit of Infinite Life and Power by stating "This Infinite Power is creating, working, ruling through the agency of great immutable laws and forces that run through all the universe, that surround us on every side. Every act of our every day lives is governed by these same great laws and forces. Every flower that blooms by the wayside, springs up, grows, blooms, and fades, according to certain great immutable laws. Every snowflake that plays between earth and heaven, forms, falls, melts, according to certain great unchangeable laws."

Trine further expresses his feeling about the subject by saying "There is nothing in the entire great universe but Law. It is continually operating, whether we are consciously aware of it or not. Natural Law is immutable, unchangeable, and permanent. Life is governed according to the natural laws and man cannot escape from it."

In *The Ascent of Man*, 1898, Henry Drummond attempts to simplify and explain evolution as steps in history. He quotes Mr. Huxley as stating that "The evolution of many existing forms of animal life from their predecessors is no longer a hypothesis but a historical fact." Drummond also understood that "All thoughts that the evolutionist works with, all theories and generalizations have been themselves evolved and are now being evolved—evolution involves not so much a change of opinion as a change in man's whole view of the world and life."

In *Life and Matter,* 1904, Sir Oliver Lodge tells us that the discussion becomes expanded into the Natural Law as the "Fundamental Cosmic Law." Lodge further expressed his understanding that the fundamental cosmic law established an "eternal persistence of matter and force and their unvarying constancy throughout the universe. All natural law is subordinate to this persistence."

The following is a further explanation of this in the form of the natural Law of Substance or the Law of Constancy. This law is a combination of two laws, namely

1. **"Chemical Law of Conservation of Matter**

   In any operation, mechanical, physical or chemical, to which matter can be subjected, its amount, as measured by weight, remains unchanged. The only way to increase or to diminish the weight of substance inside a given enclosure or geometrically closed boundary, is to pass matter in or out through the wall.

2. **Physical Law of Conservation of Energy**

   Every complete material system, even though subject to a kind of internal activity, demonstrates the fact that the total energy of the system does not change. However, that energy is either transferred or transformed. Energy can only be increased or diminished by passing a new supply of it in or out through the walls."

To these combinations, Lodge adds the Cosmological Theorems." He states that "A theorem is defined as a formula or statement embodying something to be proved from other propositions or formulas. A theorem can also be an idea, belief, method or statement generally accepted as true or worthwhile without proof. Usually, a theorem is accepted by persons persistently watching a situation under like conditions, and seeing the same results.

Cosmology is defined as the branch of philosophy dealing with the origin and general structure of the universe, with its parts, elements, and laws. It especially concerns itself with such characteristics as space, time, causality, and the general structure and evolution of the universe."

Sir Oliver Lodge relates the position taken at this point of the study by stating "We are aware that matter has always existed and that its existence is physical. However, matter is in various forms or substances. And, it is further understood that energy is the force that moves matter. Therefore, energy is referred to by some as the Spirit which is the activating and motivating force of all that exists."

Combined with the previous statements by Sir Oliver Lodge, his theories that complete the concept of cosmological theories are:

1. "The Universe or Cosmos is Eternal, Infinite and Illimitable.
2. Its substance, with its two attributes (matter and energy) fills infinite space and is in eternal motion.
3. This motion runs through infinite time as unbroken development with a periodic change from life to death, from evolution to evolution.
4. The innumerable bodies which are scattered about the space, filling the ether, all obey the same Law of Substance, Constancy or Cosmic Law—while the rotating masses slowly move towards their destruction and dissolution in one part of space, others springing into new life and development in other quarters of the universe."

In *The Mansions of Philosophy*, 1929, Will Durant documented that "We are not merely our ancestors and our circumstances; we are also wells of transforming energy, we are parts of that stream of directive force, of capacity for adaptive choice and thought, in which our forefathers also moved and had their being. These ancestors are in truth living and acting within us but the will and the life that were once in them is in each of us now, creating the 'spontaneous me.' ...will is free in so far as life is creative, in so far as it enters, with it remolding energy, as one of the determining conditions of choice and action. There is no violation of natural law in such a freedom, because life itself is a natural factor and process, not a force outside the varied realm of nature. ...Nature itself, as its fine name implies, is that living order through which all things are begotten."

Durant added "Yet there cannot be an uncaused action. Verily; but the will is part of the cause; the circumstances of an action must include the forward urgency of life. Each 'state' of mind follows naturally...the same effect always follows the same cause. But the cause is never the same...circumstances are forever changing."

In *Teachings of Silver Birch, Wisdom from the World Beyond*, 1938, he shares with us that "The universe is governed by natural laws which cannot be set aside. No guide can alter these laws or enable anyone to escape the consequences of breaking them, but he can explain them and thus help to remove the danger of ignorance. ...None escapes the Law; particularly, all who have heard the voice of the Spirit...If you learn to attune yourselves to the Law, the results will come. If the results do not come, that only proves that you are not in tune with the Law...you have the greatest riches within yourselves. You are part of the Great Spirit."

In *The Unobstructed Universe*, 1940, Stewart Edward White presented his Parallelism of Law. "There is only one set of laws but they are conditioned in two ways—as to the material they work on and the intention. Or, it can be stated that the material is the obstructed while the intention is the unobstructed." I have found this book an excellent source of research. It allows you to draw your own conclusions on the aspects of time, space, motion, frequency, conductivity and receptivity.

In *The Letters*, 1949, Joel S. Goldsmith taught that "The spiritual law is forever operative throughout the universe. It is the law of Mind; therefore, it is impersonal. In Truth there are no lies; in the consciousness of Life there is no death; in the substance of Spirit there is no matter. Limitless Mind creates only the full bloom of immediate perfection."

Time continues to move on! The Space Age is born. In 1974, Edgar D. Mitchell, an astronaut and the sixth man to walk on the moon, wrote *Psychic Exploration, a Challenge for Science.* Mitchell is also the Founder of NOETIC'S organization. He tells us that "Some areas in which outer-space research, in a synergistic blending of many disciplines, has produced benefits to inner-space research. ...A new age is rapidly emerging based on Noetics, the general study of consciousness, which will supply knowledge of the imperfectly understood subjective, psychic and spiritual side of self. The area of discovery will bring about far-reaching and rapid changes in our way of life. ...Science and technology are inundating society with inventions and knowledge about the universe that not only influence our way of living but also challenge the foundation of the social order... ."

It is obvious from the wisdom documented by Edgar Mitchell, that while our world is not changing, our understanding of it is making giant leaps forward. He concludes by telling us that "There is a need for investigators of the electromagnetic nature of man, psychologically, physiologically and the external environmental interactions. This needs to be followed by developing suitable equipment, evaluation techniques, and facilities to carry on research."

It now appears that all of the fantastic research of the 20th century has swung wide the doors of knowledge further enabling man to continue in his search in the 21st century. It is now recognized that man's consciousness is definitely in the process of expansion.

In conclusion, you will find it has been appropriate and educational for us to have reflected on the philosophers and their understanding, commencing in the early 1800s and continuing on through the present time. Let us join in this understanding

"*Amici mortui, sed magis amica veritas.*"

The meaning is that "Every law that finds expression in life is founded in wisdom, and conducive to man's happiness."

IV.

A UNIVERSAL LAW

The Golden Rule

T HERE IS A broad category of law commonly referred to as
Natural Law. It combines both the Spiritual Laws and the
Physical Laws. Science has its set of laws operating throughout the
universe, and they are better known as the physical laws. The spiritual
laws are basically concerned with our spiritual conduct and the
unfoldment or growth of our soul. These laws are often referred to as
"Laws to Live By." Although, we can list numerous laws of the
physical and of the spiritual, in reality, there is but "One" law.

As you go about your daily life, you will very quickly find that you
cannot accept one law and simply reject another law. These laws
have not been established by any religion but rather have all been
designed by the Infinite, and because of their universality they are
the foundation of democracy. When you fully understand these laws,
you can come into the understanding that because of them you can
make the best decisions applicable to your own life. You can
determine how you will handle every situation that may confront
you from time-to-time. Freedom of choice provides you with various
options. Understanding of this law, allows for you to make the best

choices. It also reveals the true meaning of "Love your neighbor as thyself."

Many of these laws are interrelated. In the chapters that follow, the laws will be outlined under two separate sections entitled "Spiritual Laws" and "Physical Laws." This format will provide a basis for a clearer understanding of the many laws within the One Law.

The Spiritual Law is our predominant topic. It is this set of laws that attend to your soul growth in your life here and hereafter. As you begin your journey into an understanding of the spiritual laws, a prerequisite is to review the familiar universal natural law—"The Golden Rule." All peoples of all societies find it equal in importance in the universe. Thus, there is a basic understanding of all philosophies, religions, and ethical systems as to how each person should treat another in a decent, kind and loving manner.

In our world today, the Golden Rule is referred to as the Law of Reciprocity. However, reciprocity had its beginning in the Golden Rule. The sages and philosophers of all times taught the Golden Rule to the masses. Down through the ages it has been presented over and over again. A word to the wise expressed by Edward Markham is

"We have committed the Golden Rule to memory; let us now commit it to life."

Keeping that thought in mind, it is suggested that you ponder upon each of the expressions of thought by the various philosophers of yesterday as well as those of today. A few items of selected scripture are included in the alphabetical listing. At the conclusion, if it is not now a part of your life, it is hoped that you will allow the Golden Rule to operate fully in your daily life from this day forth.

Aristotle
"We should behave to our friends as we would wish our friends to behave to us."

Book of Common Prayer
"My duty towards my neighbor is to love him as myself, and to do to all men as I would they should do unto me."

Einstein, Albert
"It is a very high goal free and responsible development so that he may place his powers freely and gladly in service to mankind."

Emerson, Ralph Waldo
"Every man takes care that his neighbor does not cheat him. But the day comes when he begins to care that he does not cheat his neighbor. Then all goes well."

Epictetus (Discourses, Enchiridion, Circa)
"What you would avoid suffering yourself, seek not to impose on others."

"He harms himself who does harm to another and the evil plan is most harmful to the planner."

Mahabharata
"This is the sum of all true righteousness: deal with others as thou wouldst thyself be dealt by. Do nothing to thy neighbor which thou wouldst not have him do to thee hereafter."

Milliken, Robert
"The discovery of the Golden Rule finds its beginnings in "the dawn of consciousness."

Parker, Joseph
"The Golden Rule would reconcile capitol and labor, all political contention and uproar, all unselfishness and greed."

Plato (Greece, 4ᵗʰ Century)
"May I do to others as I would that they should do unto me."

Seneca (Epistle 47:1, Roman Antiquity, 1ˢᵗ Century)
"Treat your inferiors as you would be treated by your superiors."

Shaw, George Bernard
"Do not do unto others as you would that they should do unto you. Their tastes may not be the same."

Socrates (Greece, 5ᵗʰ Century)
"Do not to others what would anger you when done to you by others."

Tobias 4:15, c. (180 B.C.)
"What thou thyself hatest, do to no man."

Tuttle, Hudson
"The first law of material is care for self; the first and fundamental law of Spirit is care for others; this Law extended in the Spirit World means "Do all for others!"

As you continue in your journey, review the pathway of the various expressions from many countries, cultures, and religions of the world. In our sharing of these teachings, it becomes clearly obvious that the feelings, around the world, appear to be mutual. It further confirms that the natural law governs us all. The various teachings of the expression which we know as the "The Golden Rule" expressed by many people in various ways are outlined below:

Native American Indian

Chief Dan George, Chief of the Salish Band, British Columbia
"We are as much alive as we keep the earth alive."

Black Elk, Holy Man of the Oglala Sioux
"All things are our relatives; what we do to everything, we do to ourselves. All is really one."

Proverb, Pima
"Do not wrong or hate your neighbor, for it is not he who wronged you, but yourself."

The Great Law of Peace
"Respect for all life is the foundation."

Anglo-American

Yahshua, Matthew 7:12 –
"Therefore, Whatsoever ye would have men to do unto you, do you even so to them: for this is the law and the prophets."

Luke 6:31 KJV –
"And as ye would that men should do to you, do ye also to them likewise."

Baha'i World Faith

Tablets of Baha'u'llah
"Ascribe not to any soul that which thou wouldst not have ascribed to thee, and that which thou doest not."

Tablets of Baha'u'llah, 71
"Blessed is he who preferreth his brother before him."

Epistle to the Son of the Wolf, 40
"And if thine eyes be turned towards justice, choose thou for they neighbor that thou choosest for thyself."

Brahmanism

Mahabharata, 5:1517
"This is the sum of duty: Do naught unto others which would cause you pain to be done to you."

Buddhism

"One should see for others the happiness one desires for himself."

Samyutta Nikaya v. 353
"A state that is not pleasing or delightful to me, how could I inflict that upon another?"

Triprtaka Udana-Varga, 5:18 - 500 B.C.
"Hurt not others in ways that you yourself would find hurtful."

<u>Chinese</u>

The Doctrine of the Mean, 13 - 500 B.C.
"What one would not wish done to himself, do not unto others."

The Doctrine of Mean
"Do not impose on others what yourself do not desire."

<u>Confucianism</u>

Analects of Confucius 15:23
"Do not do to others what you do not want done to yourself."

<u>Christianity</u>

Matthew 7:12, NKJV
"Therefore whatsoever you want to do to you, do also to them, for this is the Law and the Prophets."

<u>Egypt, Ancient</u>

The Tale of Eloquent Peasant, 109-110
"Do for one who may do for you, that you may cause him thus to do."

"He sought for others the good he sought for self; let him pass it on."

Greek, Ancient

"Do not that to a neighbor which you shall take ill from him."

Hinduism

Mahabharata 5:1517
"Do naught unto others, if be done to thee would cause pain."

Mahabharata, Anusasana Parva 113:8
"One should not behave towards others in a way which is disagreeable to one's self."

"A true act in business is to guard and do by the things others first they do by their own."

Islam

Mohammed, No. 13 of Hadith of Imam "Al-Nawawi's Forty
"None of you (truly) believes until he wishes for his brother what he wishes for himself."

"Let none of you treat his brother in a way himself would dislike being treated."

Jainism

Sutrakritanga 1.11.33
"A man should wonder about treating all creatures as he himself would be treated."

Agamas Sutrakritangas 1.10.13
"Treat all beings as he himself would be treated."

Hadith
"Not one of you truly believes until you wish for others what you wish for yourself."

Lord Mahavira, 24th Tirthankara
"In happiness and suffering, in joy and grief, we should regard as we regard our own self; and should therefore refrain from others such injury as would appear undesirable to us if inflicted on ourselves."

Acarangasutra 5.101-2
"Therefore, neither does he (a sage) cause violence to others nor does he make them do so."

Judaism

Talmud, Shabbat 31a
"What is hateful to you; do not to your fellow man. That is the whole Torah: all the rest is commentary thereof, go and learn it."

Leviticus 19:18, Torah
"Thou shalt love they neighbor as thyself."

<u>**Roman Pagan Religion**</u>

"The law imprinted on the heart of men is to love the members of society as themselves."

<u>*Persian*</u>

"Do as you would be done by."

<u>**Shintoism**</u>

"The heart of the person before you is a mirror. See there your own form."

<u>*Sikhism*</u>

"Treat others as thou wouldst be treated thyself."

Guru Arjan Devji, Sahib p. 1299
"No one is my enemy, none a stranger and everyone is my friend."

Guru Arjan Devji, Pg 259, Guru Granth Sahib
"Do not create enmity with anyone as God is within everyone."

Jupji Sahib
"Compassion, mercy and religion are the support of the entire world."

Sufism

Dr. Javad Hurbakhsh, Master of the Nimatulluhi Sufi Order
The basis of Sufism is consideration of the hearts and feelings of others. "If you haven't the will to gladden someone's heart, then at least beware lest you hurt someone's heart, for on our path, no sin exists but this."

Sunnah

"Not one of you is a believer until he desires for his brother that which he desires for self."

Taoism

Tai Shang Kan Ying P'ien 213-218
"Regard your neighbor's gain as your own gain—your neighbors loss as your own loss."

Tao The Ching, #49
"The sage has no interest of his own, but takes the interests of the people as his. He is kind to the kind; he is also kind to the unkind: for virtue is kind. He is faithful to the faithful; he is also faithful to the unfaithful: for virtue is faithful."

Zoroastrianism

Three Interpretations from Shayast-na-Shayast 13:29
"Whatever is disagreeable to yourself, do not do unto others."
"Do not do unto others whatever is injurious to yourself."
"Do not unto others all that which is not well for one's self."

Dadistan-l-Dinik, 94-95

"That nature alone is good which refrains from doing to another whatever is not good for its own self."

A conclusion on the thinkers of the ages can be expressed according to the Chinese in the Analects, 6th Century B.C.E., Confucius said:

"The entire principle can be summed up very simply in one single word "shu" which equals "reciprocity".

This review of the Golden Rule as expressed by the various prophets and people of various cultures and countries, clearly establishes that it has been knowingly, or unknowingly, recognized as the basis of all Spiritual Law. You become aware that all of the other spiritual natural laws rest upon this firm foundation; it is the solid rock. Further, it becomes very apparent that the physical laws do basically pertain to the matters of the physical world, while the spiritual law reflects to the soul, and in turn to our character and behavior. Although this is true, it is necessary to understand that the Law of Cause and Effect is very well represented in the Golden Rule. Without a doubt, the manner in which you treat your fellow man will produce an effect in your life. This is an example of the laws overlapping—the spiritual into the physical and vice versa. It is best to allow yourself flexibility in your thinking.

Always keep in mind that many of the laws have a wide scope of influence and do apply to both the physical and the spiritual realms. The spiritual laws, also known as the laws to live by, are expressed in more detail in our study than are the physical laws.

Remember, that in reality, while there are laws that apply to the physical and others that apply to the spiritual, in reality, there is no division for there is but "One Law."

V.

SEVENTY-SIX SPIRITUAL
NATURAL LAWS

The Laws to Live By

T HE LAWS THAT operate according to our level of consciousness
were expressed by Wilberforce J. Colville in his book entitled
Universal Spiritualism, 1906, as follows:

- ❖ "Iron Rule of Conduct—Bids us render evil for evil.
- ❖ Silver Rule—Counsels us to return good for good.
- ❖ Golden Rule—Urges that good be rendered in exchange for good or evil.
- ❖ Diamond Rule—Exhorts us to do all for others."

Joel S. Goldsmith, a knowledgeable writer in spiritual matters, stated
in his book *The Letters,* 1949, that "This Spiritual Law is forever
operative throughout the universe, contains no element of injustice,
knows no delay, inertia or reversal, but embodies every activity of
Divine Principle. It is the law of Infinite Life, Truth and Love,
maintaining the rule of Principle—"In earth, as it is in heaven."

"It is not by prayer and humility that you cause things to go as you wish, but by acquiring knowledge of natural law."

…Bertrand Russell

As you consider each of the Spiritual Natural Laws, an important point to remember is that they often overlap with one or more of the Physical Natural Laws. It would be correct to say that the Spiritual Laws are interrelated with the Physical Laws of the Universe. In essence, there is but One Law.

The laws are listed alphabetically. Any new law mentioned within the text of the selected law being read, will be given in detail in its correct alphabetical listing.

The Spiritual Laws

The Laws to Live By

Law of Abundance

The Law of Abundance maintains that within the universe there is a countless amount of energy. It is constantly flowing and producing sufficiency for our every desire or need.

This law is based on your ability to live in the conscious awareness of the source of all things. As you learn to recognize this oneness with the Infinite, you can manifest the law of abundance in your life. All that is, is rightfully yours!

We often hear people repeat the famous words of James Allen "As a man thinketh in his heart, so is he." This has also been expressed by Siddhartha Gautama, the Buddha "The mind is everything; what you think you become." You will find the Law of Thought is extremely helpful in the application of the Law of Abundance.

If you function in a sea of harmony with the natural law and think supply or plenty, you can succeed in the enjoyment of the fullness of life, both materially and spiritually. This will also draw more energy into your conscious awareness. As you demonstrate this law in your daily life, you will attract others to you who are seeking abundance in both the spiritual as well as in the material. In essence, we give and we receive. In turn, this brings about a collectiveness of power.

You must always remember this very important requirement—a proper intent is expected of you. Never be greedy. Your abundance should never be stashed away nor hoarded. It should always be shared. It is very necessary that a continuous flow be kept in operation. As you give, so shall you receive.

Abundance does not necessarily mean material wealth. It includes those precious things of life that money can not buy. Abundance is found in friendships, good health, happiness, joy, peace of mind, strength, relationships. The ever functioning vibrations of the unseen hold an extreme importance and value for all of us. If you refer to the material, it is a fact—you can't take it with you! Only those things that money can not buy, go with you into the life hereafter.

Spiritually, your individual consciousness is the law. In essence, you control your own abundance or supply. Very often, you become so invested in your way of life that you fret over your financial condition. You worry needlessly of how to produce more money. You may even give thought to working more hours or to finding a second job. But money should be a secondary factor. When you come into attunement with the source, you will find that you continuously produce your needs as well as your desires. Attunement is simply operating on a higher level of consciousness. Your abundance is an outer expression of your inner being. In that you are a spark of the Infinite, all that is—already is yours. Claim it!

If you give deep thought to that understanding, you will have a greater desire to help those around you who are in need. You will show more compassion, as well as be willing to assist those who do not have an understanding of the law. By demonstrating the law in your life, you are teaching others the way. When applying this law, it is extremely important that you remain positive in your thinking. If you allow any negativity to seep in, you will have to deal with the consequences (Law of Cause and Effect). The Law of Abundance blends with the Law of Prosperity, Law of Spirit of Plenty and the Law of Supply.

> "Give and it shall be given unto you; good measure, pressed down shaken together and running over; shall men give into your bosom. For with the same measure that ye mete withal, it shall be measured to you again."
>
> ∞ Holy Bible, Luke 6:38 KJV

Law of Action

The Law of Action is a state of energetic or effective activity.

Action requires energy. Any result of action is equal to the amount of energy utilized to produce it. If you use it properly, this law is able to provide for successful results in your life. It is necessary that you understand how you can use the power of thought, as well as visualization in creating the energy necessary to produce your desired results.

It is true that you may abound in various talents such as music, the arts, or politics, etc., but, unless you act on the issue at hand, there will never be a result. For instance, if your forte is playing the piano, you must sign up with a professional teacher, practice the assigned lessons, and attend your scheduled lesson period. With training and persistence, you will play the piano well. Repeated again, your positive thoughts assist you in obtaining the desired results. The greatest stumbling block to any achievement is a negative thought.

"An idea that is developed and put into action is more important than an idea that exists only as an idea."

ℰ꙳ Siddhartha Gautama, the Buddha

Law of Allowing

The Law of Allowing is the recognition of reality of that which is as well as remaining free from judging it as right or wrong simply removes any emotional attachment(s) to it.

In practicing the Law of Allowing, you learn to let things just be. You recognize that people are acting in accordance with the level of their belief system. Therefore, they make different decisions then you might make, if you were in the same circumstance. Whether their behavior is right or wrong, it is not your place to be judgmental, nor carry any of their negativity into your life. In practicing the law of allowing, you should become the observer and then make the decision as to what you want or do not want as a part of our life. It is your choice. While it is not necessary to be judgmental of another's choices or behavior, it is important to not acquire emotional attachments to them. Let them be what they will be—it's all a matter of choice. The familiar axiom "Live and Let Live" comes to mind.

Of course, the reality is that someone's actions may not be to your liking; however, it is, as it is, so just let it be! You do not need to carry the unnecessary baggage of something that you do not want into your present stage of being. At this time, it is important to activate the Law of Detachment. Rather than carry unwanted baggage, you need to turn to and activate the Law of Attraction as well as the Law of Choice. Put your energies into deliberately creating the things that you do want in your life. Simply stated, you must not give attention (energy) to that which you do not want, but give your attention (energy) to that which you want to deliberately create in your world. It is extremely important that you learn to intentionally create your desires. This process has been termed "deliberate creation." In so doing, allow others to do the same.

The Law of Allowing blends with the Law of Attraction, Law of Choice, Law of Detachment, Law of Freedom, and Law of Tolerance.

Law of Analogy

The Law of Analogy states that it is through this operation that you can trace a perfect agreement or a like correspondence between all forms of manifestation in whatsoever direction you may choose to investigate. Since no two details may be exact, there may still be some points of strong resemblance.

Here again, you should reflect back to the famous inscription on the Temple of Delphi, "Know Thyself and thou wilt know the Universe and the Gods." By a knowing and understanding of yourself, you are able to understand the Universal (God) force within yourself, as well as in the entire universe. This gives you an opportunity to apply the Law of Analogy.

In *Ancient Mystery and Modern Revelation*, 1910, Wilberforce J. Colville pointed out that "what is true of matter is likewise true of energy and mind." To give further clarity to the subject, he offers two Latin phrases:

The Hermetic axiom, "As above, so below."
Arcane Axiom Ex Uno disce Omnes, "By the discovery of one, learn thou of all."

Law of Association

The Law of Association is a constitutional affection manifested between every particle and compound in being.

The Law of Association constitutes a perfect system of order in the universe. It establishes harmony and forbids injustice. You have a task in the great scheme of the universe; however, you must find the position whereby that obligation can be met. You have the responsibility of occupying the position of life agreeable to the demands of your own nature of being. While functioning in the position you select, you must consciously consider the well-being of others.

True brotherhood can be established if the Law of Association and the Law of Affinity are fully understood and distributed appropriately. As you obtain greater awareness and understanding, you will rise to a higher position in human perception.

The Law of Association blends very closely with the Law of Influence and the Law of Affinity in that it clearly expresses that "We become like those whom we habitually admire." The whole of humanity is built on this law. In essence, you are what you are by the impressions and impact of those who surround you. Those persons whom you admire are reflected in your very being. By carefully choosing those with whom you associate, you can bring yourself into a very positive vibration. This will assist you in attuning to a higher understanding and the effect will be a raise in your consciousness.

The Law of Association blends with the Law of Affinity, Law of Attunement and Law of Influence.

> "The mind is lowered through association with inferiors. With equals it attains equality, and with superiors, superiority."
>
> ℘ Hitopadesa

Law of Attraction

The Law of Attraction suggests that the creations of like vibrations or attunement tend to be attracted to each other by a chemical affinity. This is the Law of Motion in operation. This attraction is also considered magnetic in nature as well as having a chemical affinity. There are two distinct approaches to this law:

1. Material—herein two like objects repel or are not attracted to each other
2. Spiritual—wherein two like objects attract each other.

Look around you and you will recognize that people select the company of persons with whom they are comfortable and have a mutual understanding. This law reminds us that the traits you see in others usually exist in yourself. Remember the old adages—"Birds of a feather flock together" and "You can always tell a person by the company he keeps." This is referred to as spiritual reflection. The spiritual part of man is the operating factor. You will build friendships upon how you think and act—not upon your outward appearances.

The same law governs that which you can attract from the unseen side of life. Often, you see the manifestations of this law within your own daily life. Just stop and think—you are what you think and that is exactly what you will draw unto you. It has been termed deliberate creation as well as the Law of Affinity. As you give energy to your thought, you attract to yourself that which you project—either negative or positive. It is by your actions and thoughts that you attract to yourself an inanimate control over your material and spiritual conditions. If you are not happy with your current way of life, change your thoughts and actions in order to attract that which you do desire. The Law of Thought and the Law of Suggestion play a very active part in the Law of Attraction. The Law of Attunement suggests that all like vibrations act in a magnetic way. All of these laws very closely relate to the Law of Vibration.

It is pointed out that the physical body has its own magnetic field. The terminology for that magnetic field is termed the "aura." The auric emanation of one person will affect the magnetic field of another. Have you ever walked into a room and felt a sudden surge of discomfort? As you glance around the room, you become aware of a person across the room glaring at you. Your heated argument was very recent. The result was a severe disagreement. The projection of the negative auric emanation of that individual affected you immediately upon entering the room. The Law of Attraction blends with The Law of Affinity, The Law of Attunement, Correspondence, and the Law of Influence.

"The secret of attraction is to love yourself. Attractive people judge neither themselves nor others."

                                                        ℘ Deepak Chopra

Law of Attunement

[Aligns with the Law of Harmony]

Law of Awareness

The Law of Awareness states that you become aware of what you are doing in proportion to the difficulty you experience in adapting to the current situation.

To become aware of anything, you must be conscious of it by your own perception or by information offered to you by others. You can become aware of any issue by study, investigation, listening, and being open to all avenues of information.

From the spiritual view, you choose to be aware (conscious) of the spiritual laws. You choose to raise your soul's consciousness to a higher level. These greater concepts of the universe should be incorporated into your life—mind, body and soul. You must recognize that you are not alone.

"The first step toward change is awareness. The second step is acceptance."

            ℘ Nathaniel Brandon

Law of Balance

The Law of Balance is being in complete harmony. It is a coordination of facts to a central principle as well as a reconciliation of directly opposing factors.

The Law of Balance can be referred to as coordination, even consistency, even keel, harmony, order, or lack of extremes. Balance and perfection are normal states. Once again, you should become aware that the Law of Balance overlaps between the spiritual and the physical laws.

Balance is the foundation of the universe. To operate effectively, all energy must always remain in a constant state of balance. An understanding of this Law gives you the true meaning of equilibrium. There is a counter-balancing effect within this law and through this effect an even or level state of mind can be achieved. When you have a clear understanding of this law, the gates to poise and power are opened. It is extremely important that you maintain balance in your daily life.

The Law of Balance commands that all actions of any nature between pairs of opposites in nature or between humankind must be equal—balanced! The unbalancing of any situation causes a negative reaction. For example, an unbalanced marriage may result in divorce; an unbalanced business may result in bankruptcy; an imbalance in international affairs may result in wars; and unbalanced chemicals may result in explosions, and so on.

A noted seer, The Father of The Harmonial Philosophy, gave to the world 'The Magic Staff'

> "Under all circumstances, keep an even mind. Take it; try it;
> walk with it; talk with it; lean on it; believe on it forever."
> 80 Andrew Jackson Davis

Law of Blending

The Law of Blending is the producing of a harmonious effect by intermingling of components without any line of demarcation or separateness being clearly visible.

The Law reflects in humankind when individuals come together to form a group or club in order to meet a specific goal. In your personal life, you may become attracted to a partner with likeness of mind. The two of you decide to spend your lifetime together. As time passes, you become one—blending harmoniously.

This Law reflects in all of nature and thus it expresses itself all around you as well as within you. In one instance, the universe creates its own pictures through this law. For an example, if you drive along S.R. 90 in Western New York, you would view the beautiful blue waters of Lake Erie. Or perhaps you might sit on the white sands of Daytona Beach, Florida, and view the various tones of blue of the Atlantic Ocean, white with foam. As you look off into the distance, the beautiful blue water of the lake or of the ocean seems to meet the spacious blue sky and blend in a harmonious meeting, projecting a oneness.

Perhaps, you may choose to sit on the deck of your home which is built on a mountain top in Carmel, California; it is evening and time for the sun to set. First, the blazing bright ball of sunlight projects around it various shades of red, orange and yellow, against the blue backdrop of the sky seemingly just touching the tops of the tall redwoods. Then, while all the colors around it blend in perfect harmony, the big ball of light drifts downward as it slowly sets. In the blink of the eye, it disappears. The sky slowly darkens and soon is prepared for the light of the silvery moon radiating against it. Nature, continually works in harmony with the law.

Driving through a beautiful National forest during one of the seasons of the year is another example of nature's blending process. In the springtime, you would see the various shades of green blending harmoniously as the trees and shrubs sprout anew. In the Fall, driving along the mountain tops of the Sky Line Drive of Virginia, you would view nature's painting of the various shades of green blending into a harmonious scene of yellow, orange, red, magenta, and maroon.

Another example, would be your having responded to an advertisement and purchasing tickets to listen to the music from the Big Band era. The time arrives for you to get seated in the expansive music hall; as the trumpet, trombone, violin, clarinet, flutes and drums all resound in their own tone—blending together in perfect harmony.

> "Organizational effectiveness does not lie in that narrow minded concept called rationality. It lies in the blend of clearheaded logic and powerful intuition."
>
> ℬ Henry Mintzberg

Law of Causation

The Law of Causation states that every change in nature is produced by some cause (Law of Cause and Effect) and that cause must be in harmony with the universal forces. Causation is the agency that produces an effect while causality is the regularly correlated events of phenomena. The Law of Causation and the Law of Causality are principles in Philosophy.

The Law of Causation blends with the Law of Causality.

"Conventional wisdom has always supported that when there is a crash with a large truck and a car, it is usually the car that causes the crash. If anything, this study shows the causation is more equally distributed than when we first thought."

එ Ian Grossman

Law of Cause and Effect

The Law of Cause and Effect states that every action has an appropriate reaction.

There is absolutely no exception to this law. There may be varying degrees of Cause and Effect, but absolutely nothing escapes this law. A certain cause set into motion is certain to bring a specific effect.

You set this law into motion every day, in fact every moment of the day as you think and act accordingly. The very circumstance that you create, you are forced to face. If you create joy, there is happiness; if you create sadness, there is unhappiness. This law demands that you accept full responsibility for yourself. You are always creating the cause that results in an effect in your life. If you want a situation changed, then it requires you to act accordingly.

For every effect created, you need to understand what action caused that specific effect. This gives you an opportunity to create new effects. If you create a cause, you will be assured of its just effect. The whole of life is cause and effect. Nothing happens by chance. It is the law!

The Law of Cause and Effect blends with the Law of Sequence. Since all of the laws listed below interrelate to a great degree, it will bring clarity to the subject by grouping them together under the Law of Cause and Effect. Those laws are:

    a. Law of Compensation
    b. Law of Equity
    c. Law of Karma
    d. Law of Moral Consequence
    e. Law of Retribution
    f. Law of Sequence

a. Law of Compensation

The Law of Compensation justly metes out to humankind its payment for its acts—be they good, bad or indifferent.

There is absolutely no doubt that you will reap what you sow. Nature has proven to be the great harmonizer and the balancing factor of the universe. Whatever the case, this law automatically exerts itself for reward or punishment distributions. Frankly speaking, "you get back exactly what you give out." If you render a service, you will receive a just and positive payment; if you injure another, you will receive a just negative payment. This law responds to the choices you make in your daily life. The choices you make are building your resulting karma.

There are times when this law is not adequately understood. Very often, you may hear a person say, "I see people transgressing or sinning all the time. Yet, they get by so very well. Just look at me, I am trying to do everything right and to the very best of my ability, yet everything goes wrong. The law simply isn't functioning properly. It's not fair."

There are two errors in this thinking. First, this kind of thinking denotes a severe state of negativity. Secondly, it should be understood that this law is not based on your observing the payment another receives for his deeds or misdeeds. That issue does not matter, for the law operates in perfect order and in perfect timing.

Remember, that you must pay for the errors you make, knowingly or unknowingly, along your way. You are rewarded for all the goodness you do as well as for the conformity with natural law that you demonstrate in your life. This law clearly shows that the Infinite Source (God, Great Spirit, etc.) is no respecter of persons.

The Law of Compensation blends with the Law of Equity and the Law of Retribution.

> "Compensation is payment for service rendered or injury suffered."
>
> ∞ Ralph W. Emerson

b. Law of Equity

The Law of Equity is a condition of being just, impartial, and fair.

The Law of Equity gives to humankind its just due. It does not matter whether you agree, disagree, remain neutral or whether you are even aware of it. It does prevail! Undoubtedly, the purpose of the Law of Equity (The Law of Trust) is to equip each of us with a moral philosophy that will stand the test of every assault that could ever be made upon it. Simply stated, you will receive according to what you have earned. It is a simple and just compensation. This law clearly is associated with the Law of Cause and Effect and the Law of Compensation.

It is important for you to understand that knowledge brings responsibility. As you come into a greater understanding of all the laws, you also accept a greater responsibility for living in accordance with that new understanding.

> "There is but one law for all, namely, that law which governs all law, the law of our Creator, the law of humanity, justice, equity—the law of nature and of nations."
>
> ✆ Edmund Burke

c. Law of Karma

The Law of Karma governs the balance of energy within our system of morality. Its basis is the law of cause and effect. It is also referred to as the law of moral causation.

This law is the universal teacher of responsibility. If the law is properly understood, it can give meaning to the retribution you have to make or the just compensation you will receive. This is the natural principle of Cause and Effect. Every action will have its karmic reaction.

Many adherents of karma say that you are currently living under karmic debt from a past life. While this may be a fact, you are absolutely free to choose how you will meet and pay any debt that you have incurred. Freedom of will prevails under karma. The consequences of your choices set this law into action. It is wise to not allow any negative influences of your past influence your present; and, certainly do not let them influence your future.

Always remember that karma does bring forth reward as well as punishment—it all depends on what you have created in your thoughts or in your actions. The universal accounting system is accurate and without error. It calculates your ledger clearly and accurately. This is a demonstration of the Law of Balance. Without a doubt, you can be assured that you will receive in full measure from the universe that which you have given to it.

The Law of Karma blends with the Law of Compensation, Law of Equity, and Law of Retribution.

> "As the blazing fire reduces wood to ashes, similarly, the fire of Self-knowledge reduces all karma to ashes."
>
> ఴ Bhagavad-Gita

d. Law of Moral Consequence

The Law of Moral Consequence states good is returned for good, evil is returned for evil.

The Law of Moral Consequence consists of all that has been written in the Laws of Cause & Effect, Law of Compensation, Law of Equity, Law of Karma, Law of Retribution, Law of Trust, and the Law of Sequence. The law follows in a succession of consequences collectively here and individually hereafter. It is the old axiom, "As a man sows, so he shall reap." As you act and interact with others in your daily life, it requires you to not only quote The Golden Rule but to put it into practice by demonstrating it in the way you live. Always, "Do unto others as you would have them do unto you."

e. Law of Sequence

The Law of Sequence includes all activity grouped under the general heading of the Law of Cause and Effect and demonstrated in succession.

This is the Karmic Law as well as the Law of Retaliation. Nothing ever occurs simply by chance. There must be and there definitely is an efficient precedent for every consequence. There is a regular sequence or orderly procession of all the phenomena in the universe. Nothing in our universe stands alone. No act can be totally isolated. Every act follows a thought and precedes the appropriate sequence of events that follow.

> "The events in our lives happen in a sequence in time, but in their significance to ourselves they find their own order: the continuous thread of revelation."
>
> ℠ Eudora Welty

Law of Choice

The Law of Choice can be termed the engine of our evolutionary process.

Choice can be defined as an option, a preference, or a selection. By your choices, you create the cause and effect in your life. By choice, you also bring the Law of Attraction and Law of Allowing into play. Responsible choices take into account the consequences you must face based on that choice.

In his book entitled *Seat of the Soul*, Gary Zukav emphasizes that:

"Temptation is the gracious way of introducing the soul to his own power...right choices bring right results."

As you investigate the evolutionary process of your life, it requires that you examine your soul and its growth. When you seek growth of your soul, you are able to attune to the higher vibrations within and as a result you become more intuitive. You then elevate yourself from the five senses into a broader scope of being and that awareness includes the sixth sense. This is commonly referred to as spiritual evolution.

The Law of Choice blends with Law of Allowing, Law of Attraction and the Law of Freedom.

"Nobody can go back and start a new beginning, but anyone can start today and make a new ending."

                ഔ Maria Robinson

Law of Conscience

The Law of Conscience is the guiding light within each of us. It sets a moral or ethical judgment to one's behavior, whether it is in their thoughts or deeds.

Everyone is born with a conscience. That faculty must be nurtured from birth in order for it to come into the proper alignment. A child does not automatically know right from wrong. It is extremely important for parents to teach the child right from wrong at the earliest possible stage of the child's capability to understand. The conscience can become the child's guide once the child begins to accept responsibility for its own behavior. It is necessary to "bring up a child in the way he shall go, and when he is old he will not depart from it."

As we continue to grow, we should continue to nurture our conscience. Your own conscience is your chamber of justice. It is the policeman of your life. The conscience is a sensitive evaluator of your morals and it compels you to do what is right and proper at all times.

The conscience is often referred to as the 'still small voice within' ever reminding you of right and wrong. How often have you heard it said, "Let your conscience be your guide?" If you have nurtured your soul (conscience) along the way, you can listen to that still small voice within. It will never allow you to think wrong or do wrong. Conscience is the basis of alertness, creativity, efficiency, happiness, health, and organizational power. A clear conscience gives one inner peace. Meditate on the words of these five great teachers:

"Conscience is God's deputy in the soul."

ဢ Rev. T. Adams

"Conscience is a great ledger book in which all our offences are written and registered, and which time reveals to the sense and feeling of the offender."

ဢ Burton

"Conscience is that faculty which perceives right and wrong in actions, approves or disapproves them, anticipates their consequences under the moral administration of God and is thus either the cause of peace or disquietude of mind."

ဢ Rev. S. Conn, D.D.

"Be fearful only of thyself; and stand in awe of none more than thine own conscience. There is a Cato in every man: a severe censor of his manners. And he that reverences this judge will seldom do anything he need repent of."

                                    ℅ Fuller

"A man of integrity will never listen to any reason against conscience."

                                    ℅ Home

It is extremely important that you understand the conscience and its value in your life. When you are aware of this interior guide, you may also recall the words of Socrates when he said: "Know thyself and thou wilt know the Universe and the Gods."

Do you remember the axiom, "You can fool some of the people some of the time but you can't fool all the people all the time?" Your conscience knows exactly what you are doing; and, it also knows what you are thinking of doing. It truly is your unseen guide. Your conscience is the voice of your higher self—the inner sense perception. It is your policeman that never takes leave of his duty. A wise expression of an ancient sage is: "Wherever you consciousness is, you are!"

Law of Continuity

The Law of Continuity emphasizes that there is never a break in nature. Absolutely nothing passes from one state to another without passing through all the intermediate stages of existence. The Law of Continuity and the Law of the Invisible and the Visible are principles in Philosophy.

This statement of the Law of Continuity is referring to a process that is termed the Law of Evolution. This law actually clarifies for us that the natural law does not stop with the visible (the physical) and then give place to a new set of laws for the invisible (spiritual laws). The Law of the Invisible (Spiritual) and the Law of the Visible (Physical) are both within the Law of One.

It is necessary to understand that these laws cover the spectrum from the Law of Matter through the Law of the Spiritual. In this understanding, you will find the law is the revelation of time. The law alone is the constant authority.

Henry Drummond clearly stated "This law furnishes us an "a priori argument" for the position we are attempting to establish of the most convincing kind—final. It has been said it is the expression of Divine Veracity of Nature—for the universe obeys and behaves. This law puts the finishing touch to the harmony of the universe. As we study the law, we find few exact definitions of it but rather a multitude of exhibitions of the law and its operation within the universe. It is difficult for the thinking man to conceive of a set of principles (rules) to guide him through his natural life and at a certain point (death of the physical) suddenly find himself subject to a new set of laws. Nature does not provide for such confusion. The law has been demonstrated in the plant, animal and mineral kingdoms. The sciences have created departments and specialization to facilitate its own scale of intelligence but by no means intends to break the continuity of an evolving universe."

Drummond continues his explanation, "The greatness of the law leaves its final impression on the mind in regard to uniformity of nature. This law gives us an understanding of the continuity of life and the continuous existence of the soul."

The Law of Continuity blends with the Law of Invisible and the Law of Visible.

> "The Universe is a unity and trinity. It is made up of Spirit, Force and Matter. Spirit contains force and force contains matter. Thus, matter can be destroyed but the force being higher cannot be destroyed and it is the substance that contains Spirit—thus, life with no end."
>
> ℘ Wilberforce J. Colville

Law of Correspondence

The Law of Correspondence provides that the internal of any object—whether person, thought or thing is ever represented in the external and vice versa.

This Law operates completely in that it manifests its unceasing operation everywhere in our universe. It becomes obvious, that you cannot logically deny those things in affinity. Andrew J. Davis explained it in these terms "Literally, the internal and external are united; thus correspond to each example, trees correspond to the tree of knowledge; gold to the celestial goodness; silver to spiritual truth."

The Law of Correspondence between the spiritual and material is wonderfully exact in its operation. When you create a thought, you will receive the corresponding element. If you dwell on sadness, the attraction will be corresponding sadness. If you are cheerful, without a doubt you are subject to other cheerful elements in your life. In understanding this law, be aware of the overlapping of the Law of Attraction, Law of Cooperation and the Law of Thought.

This Law is clearly one of the bridges between the seen and the unseen. While we are aware there are planes of existence beyond our current understanding, we also know that the Law of Correspondence is present throughout the universe. Therefore, by analogy we can assume a similarity of other planes of existence. The old axiom "As above, so below; as below, so above" takes on new meaning. This principle allows man to reason intelligently from the known to the unknown, basically using the Law of Analogy.

One of the cosmic principles is "there is always a correspondence between the laws and phenomena of the various planes of life and being. Therefore we become aware that everything has substance/ body, motion/energy and definitely conscious awareness." In reality, all external things exist in an invisible condition and the recognized form is the manifestation of its inward reality. The Law of Correspondence is demonstrated as an agreement between manifestations.

The Law of Correspondence blends with the Law of Affinity, Law of Attraction, Law of Cooperation and the Law of Thought.

> "As the bodily form expresses the character of man's spirit, so also the works of his hands declare his inward nature."
>
> ∞ Emanuel Swedenborg

Law of Creation

The Law of Creation is the bringing into existence and so it is.

Creation is the effect and results from the cause, which is thought. Every thought, coupled with emotion, has the power to create reality. Thought provides the avenue to think and act and results in creation.

The underlying law of creation is a rhythmic (Law of Rhythm) balanced (Law of Balance) interchange. It exists in all of nature.

To go a step further into a higher understanding, ponder this thought as expressed in the great works of Walter Russell when he stated:

"Inspired man alone can create enduring things. To create we must first conceive. To conceive we must stop thinking and KNOW...the language of this communion is a language of light called inspiration."

As a human being, you are Spirit in like image of your Source. You have the capability of creating. Your thoughts put into action create things. In *A New Beginning* by Jerry & Ester Hicks, they define the Law of Creation in the simple terms of "Intend (want) it, and allow it to be—and it is." Our understanding also makes it clear that there is continuity in creation, and that creating force is always in motion.

The Law of Creation blends with the Law of Allowing and the Law of Fulfillment.

> "The creation of the universe was not simply an initiatory act but is in continual operation." …Everyone who thinks from clear reason sees that the universe was not created out of nothing, because he sees that it is impossible for anything to be made out of nothing: for nothing is nothing, and to make anything out of nothing is contradictory, and what is contradictory is against the light of Truth, which is from the Divine Wisdom. …Everyone who thinks from clear reason sees also that all things have been created out of substance which is substance in itself, for this is the very Esse out of which all things that are, can exist and because the Infinite

alone is Substance in itself, and thence the very Esse, it is evident that the existence of things has no other source."

           ℘ Emanuel Swedenborg

Law of Cycles

The Law of Cycles expresses a universal circular direction of process or progress.

Following a circular direction is expressed through the Law of Rhythm, which creates recurring movement. There is a constant cycle of birth, growth, death and new life that flows in a circular motion— all things must begin and end at the same point. For example, in your daily existence, you awaken in the morning to the light of day. You also have a time period in which you may work or apply effort in some manner. As evening comes, you can relax and enjoy your family. In order to regenerate your mind and body, darkness provides time for sleep. As morning approaches, you awaken to daylight and begin again.

Likewise nature displays cycles by the seasons of year continuing as spring, summer, fall, and winter. They never change in their placement for they operate in a cycle. Electrons in the atoms move in circles. The planets and the sun move in circles. In philosophy, you can often witness the old being renewed. In scientific studies, you find that trends return. Today, there is a revival of soul-searching as well as a revival in the study of psychic phenomena—another cycle.

The Law of Cycles seems to prove to be the principle or regulator for timing the events and operations of everything, the visible and invisible, in mind and in matter, in time, and in space. We observe the rise and fall of nations and are aware that civilizations pass away.

Those who accept the teachings of reincarnation are aware of the cycle of life—physical birth and physical death—the soul awakening in a higher realm to grow in knowledge and truth. Once again, with good reason and courage, the soul can choose to return to earth for yet another series of earth's lessons.

A study of the Law of Cycles brings to light that various cultures and orders teach this law as a basic universal law. For instance, in Greece, it was believed each cycle repeated the characteristics of its predecessor. It appears the Law of Cycles embodies a scientific, philosophic, and religious basis for a comprehensive philosophy of life itself. This Law is closely related to the Law of Rhythm and the Law of Vibration.

The Rosicrucian doctrine concerning cyclicity is that "A swinging pendulum (free to move in any direction) is subjected to the conflicting attractions and repulsion of other manifestations of force and energy, then there is manifested the universal tendency toward the circular trend—the tendency to convert the straight path of the swing into a circular path or cycle."

No matter what the past has been, every day is a new beginning for all. Life goes on and the wheels keep turning!

The Law of Cycles blend with the Law of Rhythm.

> "There seems to be a kind of order in the universe, in the movement of the stars and the turning of the earth and changing of the seasons, and in the cycle of human life."
>
> ᛋᚩ K. Anne Porter

Law of Desire

The Law of Desire is the natural want or intention to seek knowledge and to comprehend all that is within the universe.

It is through desire that you expand your awareness. It is a fact that the more you become attuned to Nature, the more creative you can become. You are encouraged to understand how the Law of Attraction, Correspondence, Intention and Thought blend with the Law of Desire.

The Law of Desire is the power which drives your physical as well as your spiritual self while the will remains the directional force. In this material world, you can attract whatever you desire, if you so choose. The quality of the desire underlies the process. You will attract exactly whatever you expect to receive. Thus, it is necessary that you utilize the proper thought process. Napoleon Hill taught: "There is one quality which one must possess to win, and that is definiteness of purpose, the knowledge of what one wants, and a burning desire to possess it."

If your desires and your expectations are not in agreement, you are a house divided. You cannot desire wealth and think or express poverty in your thoughts or in your verbal statements. You cannot desire positive effects while you continually think and act in the negative mode. You must be of one mind and of one accord. If you structure one mindedness, you will raise your consciousness and allow the movement of energy into a balanced condition. However, if you allow doubt and fear to enter your well-being, you bar all of the positive effects.

Your sincere desire, along with expectation, can bring you fulfillment. You must fully understand that every desire fed with proper intention has the means within itself to bring your every dream into reality. This law is the basis of evolution, of life, and of truth.

The Law of Desire blends with the Law of Choice and the Law of Intention.

"You can have anything you desire—if you want it badly enough. You can be anything you want to be, do anything you set out to accomplish if you hold to that desire with singleness of purpose."

                                                 ∾ Abraham Lincoln

Law of Detachment

The Law of Detachment declares in order to acquire anything in the physical universe, you have to let go of your attachment to it.

Attachment can be explained as "an affinity, bond, fondness, or even the love for something." Attachment can be totally emotional. Detach can best be explained as "a separating from something." You may eliminate unwanted baggage in your life by practicing the Law of Detachment. In a specific situation, it might be said that you are not concerned or do not care. This is not true. You simply have decided not to participate emotionally. You are allowing whatever will be to unfold. You basically are accepting the unknown. A recent quote is: "If you love something, let it go for if it is meant for you, it will return to you." When you are secure within and you know yourself, there is ease in practicing this Law.

When allowing yourself to be attached, you tend to follow a set pattern or routine. Why is this so? It is simply, because it seems safe and secure. When you release that routine or face change, you face the unknown. In many cases, this state of mind brings about uncertainty. While it may be uncomfortable at first, learning to let go opens the doorway to allow many more enjoyable and profitable possibilities come into your life.

Buddha is quoted as saying: "It is your resistance to what is that causes your suffering." You must learn to accept the now, change what you need to change and be wise enough to accept people, things, and situations for what they represent. This allows freedom for all. Once you learn to accept this concept you can be involved, yet remain detached.

When you practice detachment, you also allow those around you to be themselves. You do not require them to react to your perception of things. In practicing detachment, you do not impose your solution or input as to the manner of handling of another's situation. You allow others freedom in resolving their own issues.

Make no mistake; this does not interfere with the Law of Desire or the Law of Intention. If you commit your self to the law, energies result allowing you the freedom to be who you are and it also allows those around you the choice of being who they choose to be. The law cautions that you not allow yourself to be conditioned by another's way of thinking. Unless you practice the Law of Detachment, you will cause your power of creativity to stymie. By not practicing this Law, you limit your well-being.

The Law of Detachment aligns with the Law of Allowing.

"Those who are attuned to Truth remain balanced and detached forever."

         ℘ Sri Guru Granth Sahi

Law of Divine Order

[Aligns with the Law of Orderly Trend]

Law of Equity

[Aligns with the Law of Cause and Effect]

Law of Evolution

Since the Law of Evolution applies equally to the Spiritual and the Physical, and since it is understood and accepted in the sciences, it has been placed in the next section listing the Physical Laws.

Law of Example

The Law of Example decrees that any human being, concept or thing which is placed in a position of significance may well serve as an example (pattern) for others to follow.

Webster defines example as "one that serves as a pattern to be imitated or not to be imitated." In that line of thought, the simple axiom "Teach them by showing them" comes to mind.

If you are to be a leader, you must demonstrate fairness, harmony, love, patience, peace, and the Golden Rule. The greatest demonstration must be displayed with humility and in being of service. Einstein once said "Example isn't another way to teach, it is the only way to teach." A leader, whose ego takes control, becomes the petty tyrant Carlos Castaneda describes so very well in many of his books. You will lose your status as a leader, when you become self-important. You will also find that you are no longer a good example for others to follow.

> "He that gives good advice, builds with one hand; he that gives good counsel and example, builds with both; but he that gives good admonition and bad example, builds with one hand and pulls down with the other."
>
> ℘ Francis Bacon, Sr.

Law of Fear

The Law of Fear prescribes that an unpleasant emotion causes alarm or an anticipation of danger. It is a negative and most destructive force in your consciousness.

The power of thought plays an important roll in the operation of this law. You have been taught that what you think becomes a part of you. If you continually hold a negative thought involving a fear, you remain in a state of awaiting that fear to manifest and become reality. This is a demonstration of Cause and Effect. The Cause was the fear and the effect will be that which results.

Negative thinking creates all of the things you do not want as a part of your life. You must continue to accentuate the positive and eliminate the negative in your thinking; all fears will then dissipate. M. Ferguson said: "Ultimately we know deeply that the other side of fear is freedom." In understanding the Natural Law, you must recognize the effects that you receive result from the cause that you chose. You create your own fears. To rid yourself of fear, you must create courage by cultivating positive thoughts.

"You can conquer almost any fear if you will only make up your mind to do so. For remember, fear doesn't exist anywhere except in your mind."

ဆာ Dale Carnegie

Law of Flexibility

The Law of Flexibility is the practical acceptance of what is taking place in one moment in time.

This law requires that you be alert and make constructive use of the moment; for in the twinkling of an eye, all things may change. If you are flexible, you can and will adapt to any change that is necessary. In simple terms, to be flexible you graciously accept change. Some times change seems to present a problem. Always remember to be flexible; recognize that a problem is nothing more than a challenge. It is an opportunity that you did not have a moment ago.

"There are two types of minds—the mathematical, and what may be called the intuitive. The former arrives at its views very slowly but they are firm and rigid; the latter is endowed with greater flexibility and applies itself simultaneously to the dive."

ဆာ Blaise Pascal

Law of Forgiveness

The Law of Forgiveness expresses the necessity of allowing bygones to be bygones.

In essence, you must let go of all resentments of the past as well as the present. By doing so, you are not allowing resentments to retard your own spiritual growth. As long as you hold on to resentment, you are binding that very vibratory rate to you. You must let go of all resentment. By forgiving, you remove all guilt from the one who has created a negative force in your life. You can also remove or release all guilt concerning someone who has made their transition into the world beyond. You can create a positive correspondence in the vibrations between the two worlds—the seen and unseen. When practicing the Law of Forgiveness, you are demonstrating that you have raised your own vibration to a Spirit of Love. You no longer hold malice for a deed another has committed against you or that you have committed to another. You are practicing the Golden Rule and in turn creating a true brotherhood.

As you forgive, you are creating a vibration of harmony. You should be aware that while you may have forgiven others, it is very necessary that you ask forgiveness from others for any wrongs you may have committed knowingly or unknowingly. In like manner, a very significant point is that you must learn to forgive yourself.

Henry W. Beecher reminded us that we must forgive and forget, and he said "I can forgive, but I cannot forget, is only another way of saying I cannot forgive. Forgiveness should be like a canceled note—torn in two, burned up, so that it can never be shown against one."

Only good can come from forgiveness. Forgiving is a simple act of creating a balance where an imbalance once existed. If injustice is replaced, it can no longer become a part of your life. If you hold on to this negative force, it becomes real and active in your life. It can cause stumbling blocks in your pathway in the journey of life. The natural law forces you to work through every situation. If you work in the energy of forgiveness, you create a greater understanding of your spiritual lessons.

"Sincere forgiveness isn't colored with expectations that the other people apologize or change. Don't worry whether or not they finally understand you. Love them and release them. Life feeds back truth to people in its own way and time."

ॐ Sara Paddison

Law of Freedom

The Law of Freedom is the power of deliberate unlimited choice.

This is a very important and a very powerful law. It makes you aware of the power that is within you. It is necessary to recognize that you are free only to the degree that you understand there is no power outside of yourself. Once this is accepted, you have full recognition of your own power of choice in all that you do.

It is a basic fact that you can choose your way of life (Law of Choice). You can desire to progress and take such action as necessary or you can limit yourself to suffering, unhappiness, and status quo. It depends solely on how the Law of Freedom and the Law of Choice is practiced in your life. You have the freedom to make your own decisions whether they are right or wrong, correct or incorrect. As you give consideration to this law, you may find there is not necessarily a wrong way but perhaps just a detour in your pathway that is allowing for more growth through new experiences.

You have the freedom to allow others to have their own way of thinking and living as well. The law guarantees you the opportunity for choice—the right to choose your own path in life to follow. It is another great teacher when combined with the Laws of Allowing, Compensation, Detachment, Karma, and Understanding. You can choose to be set free from all bondage and from all error. No other person can ever take power over your destiny, unless you allow it.

The Law of Freedom opens the door. It gives you the opportunity to approach life's situations in a positive manner. It grants you the pathway which offers you the ability to change any situation, if you so choose.

The Law of Freedom blends with the Law of Allowing and the Law of Choice.

> "Every human has four endowments: self-awareness, conscience, independent will, and creative imagination. These give us the ultimate freedom...the power to choose, to respond, and to change."
>
> හ Stephen R. Covey

Law of Free Will

The Law of Free Will establishes that no matter what conditions, circumstances, or challenges prevail in your life, you have the ability and power to choose your own pathway in your journey through life.

This Law sustains the fact that you will always have options (Law of Choice). You can choose to submit to the direction of others or you may choose to take the lead. In essence, you can be the sheep or the shepherd; it is your choice under this Law. Your creative thoughts and actions can either build or destroy. Free will allows you to be the creator of your life. The capability of having your own thought is an example of free will.

If you accept the philosophy of predestination, be aware that it is you and only you who have the option of fulfilling that destination or opting for another. You make the choice of how Free Will operates in your own life.

"The robber of your free will," writes Epictetus, "does not exist."

                                   ℾ Marcus Aurelius

"Free will and determinism are like a game of cards. The hand that is dealt you is determinism. The way you play your hand is free will."

                                   ℾ Norman Cousins

Law of Fulfillment

[Aligns with the Law of Creation]

Law of Giving

The Law of Giving validates a continuous flow and that flow results in the creation of another cycle.

The phrase is often repeated, "As you give, so you shall receive." This creates a perpetual flow of energy in motion. Since the Law of Constancy and Law of Sequence are always in effect, you know that the universe is never in a static condition. It has been proven time and time again that the more you give, the more you will receive. There is also a proper way to give; and, that is to give freely and willingly. If you give in any other manner expecting something in return, it is abominable; and, it creates a stumbling block in your receiving a blessing.

If you think in terms of money, you must realize that it is useless to hoard it. Hoarding stops the flow. And if the flow is stopped, nothing can be returned to you. Your intent is very important if you are to create the good that flows continuously. J. Rohn expressed it so very well when he said that "Giving is better than receiving, because giving starts the receiving process."

Giving is not necessarily of a material nature. In giving, there are far more important things in life than money. Your intention or desire to be a blessing to humankind should be the principal priority. Along life's path, you may meet an individual who simply needs a kind word, a compliment, a smile, a pat on the back, or maybe the kind words "thank you for all that you do for others." Sometimes, a simple act of kindness expressing that you care is sufficient. When you give, it is important that you do so with the proper attitude and intent. Develop the practice of giving a smile to everyone you pass each day along life's highway. Just a simple, little smile may be a saving grace for that individual. Love is the answer for opening the door to a better you.

"The human contribution is the essential ingredient. It is only of the giving of one's self to others that we truly live."

&) E. P. Andrus

Law of Gratitude

The Law of Gratitude is a principle expressing that action and reaction are always equal in opposite directions.

Basically, the law is clear in cause and effect (action and reaction). The Law of Gratitude is a demonstration of thankfulness and appreciation. This practice activates the Law of Abundance; as you give, so shall you receive. As you practice this Law, you are in a state of being appreciative and thankful. In being grateful, you will find that you are functioning in a vibration of a very strong positive energy.

Every day you are given many opportunities to give thanks for the many positive things in your life. It is also good to give thanks for what the stumbling blocks (negatives) that fell in your pathway have taught you. Always give thanks for the past and the enlightenment it has given to you. Be thankful for the present in which you can demonstrate the knowledge you have gleaned and prepare for the greatness of your future. It is wise to remember that sincere gratitude is a powerful tool for creating abundance in your life. If you neglect to offer gratitude, it has been found that life can become difficult.

A sincere expression of gratitude to anyone who has given to you creates a positive vibration for both persons. Elizabeth Bibesco reminds us that: "Blessed are those who can give without remembering and take without forgetting." No matter whether gratitude is extended materially or spiritually, the thanks given to the giver is a stimulant of peace and joy within. A grateful mind is fixed upon the eternal law of increase. Increase or abundance, is the return given for gratitude expressed.

"He who receives a good turn should never forget it; he who does one, should never remember it."

ဆ Charron

"Gratitude bestows reverence, allowing us to encounter everyday epiphanies, those transcendent moments of awe that change forever how we experience life and the world."

ဆ John Milton

Law of Harmony

The Law of Harmony is the condition of being in one accord, perfect attunement.

The Laws of Attunement, Balance, Rhythm, Polarity and the Law of Vibration are very closely related to the Law of Harmony. Vibration, Rhythm, and Harmony are motion. All motion within the universe is dominated by a particular flowing order (Law of Sequence). Any action of Rhythm or Vibration carries an abundance of power. This particular flowing order produces the various manifestations of the universe. While everything is in a state of vibration, it is rhythmic consistency that produces a specific manifestation.

The key to awareness of harmony is to understand how to regulate the rate of vibration—thus, changing the motion or rhythm and producing an orderly, harmonious flow. In so doing, it is important to be aware that your thoughts are very powerful and do create an energy field. This energy field can result in maintaining harmony or in creating unbalance. Be very careful what you think!

As indicated, the Law of Vibration is also considered an intricate part of the Law of Harmony. This is evident in the fact that this law expresses that all things in the universe exist in various states of motion (harmony).

In your daily life, you may be anxious to bring something into fruition. You work hard and put a lot of effort into your project. When nothing happens, it seems you have hit a stone wall. If you review the situation, there is no doubt that you were not working in a harmonious vibration at all. Your impatience of the results slowly manifesting may be part of the problem. Relax and go with the flow.

If you take the time to come into a rapport with the natural laws of the universe, you just may find things will work out to your benefit and without a lot less effort.

"Harmony is pure love, for love is complete agreement."

80 Lope de Vega

"He who lives in harmony with himself lives in harmony with the universe."

80 Marcus Aurelius

Law of Healing

The Law of Healing is the channeling of positive, powerful energy radiating from the Source into the mind or body of one that is diseased (dis-eased). We define disease as lacking in ease.

Energy (motion) improves health conditions by removing disease and creating an ease in the condition (Law of Balance) which then may result in a complete healing of the physical body. Positive healing energy is able to correct both physical conditions as well as afflictions of the mind.

Healing may occur in the presence of the healer. The energy field or the healing energies may also be transmitted to a person at a distant location; either method may offer good results.

Today, the laying-on-of-hands has become a common and practical method of transmitting the energy from one human being to another. In other methods of healing, (e.g. Reiki, Kinetic, and Cranial) the energy is moved about the body; and, in some cases without the need of necessarily touching the body. Another method is directing energy to the particular chakra that is afflicted. Regardless of the process utilized, energy directed from the Infinite Source flowing through the healer to the patient, promotes healing in the patient whether the patient is present or absent. The methods of practicing healing are many and vary among different groups of practitioners. Every healer must practice to find the method best suited to their own energy field.

In this light, you must also understand that spiritual healing may be a product of extending your empathy to one in need emotionally or spiritually. It has been found that very often empathy serves well in the healing process. You should welcome any request for healing, no matter what the nature may be—physical, mental or spiritual. To be a healer is an opportunity to be of service to your fellow human beings.

"Natural forces within us are the true healers of disease."

ॐ Hippocrates

Law of Humility

The Law of Humility demonstrates the act of submissive respect.

The Law of Humility is best described as being the servant of humankind. To be humble is an attribute to be sought. One way to learn humility is through the practicing of this law. The more spiritually inclined you tend to be, the more selflessness that you will display. Proverbs 16:18 (KJV) states that: "Pride goeth before destruction and a haughty spirit before the fall."

It is important that you understand that when practicing the law of humility, you are not required to become the whipping board for another. However, it does require that you have an attitude of modesty as well as that of being respectful and considerate of others.

Humility brings about a sense of compassion toward the struggles others are having in their lives. Humility projects a clear demonstration of understanding, caring, and being involved in humankind. It also demonstrates a state of selflessness. The inner being of one's spirituality is demonstrated outwardly as being the servant for the unseen.

> "Humility is the foundation of all the other virtues hence, in the soul in which this virtue does not exist there cannot be any other virtue except in mere appearance."
>
> ഇ St. Augustine

Law of Indirectness

The Law of Indirectness expresses that a thought can be put out of the mind, easier and more successfully by throwing the mind on to some other object or thing.

It has been proven that an attempt to remove something from your mind by dwelling upon it, does not get the desired result. You can inject another thought into your mind and in doing so change your mind's direction. This new thought, tossed into your mind, will become all absorbing. Although you may be unaware of this technique, it is a common practice. For instance, your mind comes into play when you are attempting to lose weight by dieting. The thought of food is forever taking over your mind. It becomes apparent that you cannot lose weight because you are constantly nibbling. When this occurs, it is necessary to practice the Law of Indirectness by placing another non-related thought into your mind. Your mind will promptly absorb the new thought.

This same formula may be utilized when you desire to change or break a habit. In order to break a habit, you must toss a thought of something totally non-related into your mind. This change may be by thought or by action, such as getting involved in doing something else. This practice is simply a means of diverting attention to an issue or situation.

Another instance where the Law of Indirectness may be utilized is when a situation arises that causes you to become angry, hateful, revengeful or just simply upset over a situation. If this occurs, you must simply throw your mind on to another object or thought, resulting in a change of vibration. When you continue to use this method, your mind will quickly learn to always redirect when necessary.

Law of Influence

[Aligns with the Law of Affinity and the Law of Attraction]

Law of Intention

[Aligns with the Law of Desire]

Law of Intuition

The Law of Intuition is the faculty of knowing or sensing without rational processing.

Webster defines Intuition as "the power or faculty of attaining to direct knowledge or cognition without evident rational thought and inference." Intuition is an innate ability that we all were freely given at birth. Developing it to its fullest capability is our own responsibility.

Your intuition will be your constant guide when you are willing to raise your level of consciousness. Entering the silence and meditating daily, are keys to accomplishing this new level of understanding. Your inner being will produce the guidance or information you need or desire. The universal force will assist you in utilizing your intuition. However, if you continue to depend upon or continue to seek the guidance you need from others, your intuition can not function properly.

In our busy world, some individuals turn to others to assist them in solving issues of their lives. They allow counselors, ministers, psychologists, etc. to guide them in a path that will hopefully bring them the peace and security they seek. Many people become dependent on sources outside of themselves. In many cases, it becomes clear to the professional that it would be of value to teach their client how to use their own intuition.

It is extremely important to teach you how to turn within and raise your own vibratory rate. If you practice meditation and entering the silence daily, you will change your level of consciousness to a higher vibration. This will result in an increase in your spirituality and your inner being (conscience). Once the conscience is trained, it will always guide and direct you in a positive manner. Chapters VIII & IX offer you guidance in the pathway of unfoldment.

"Intuition comes very close to clairvoyance; it appears to be the extrasensory perception of reality."

                                                    ℘ Alexis Carrel

Law of Invisible

[Aligns with the Law of Continuity]

Law of Justice

The Law of Justice gives to every man his just due impartially and equitably.

The scales of justice rest in balance (Law of Balance). All things must be in proper order (Law of Orderly Trend) to maintain a true balance. Truth is the foundation of justice. The Law of Justice is a birthright and remains such throughout your life on earth. You can freely claim its protection.

While you recognize justice that is instituted by our society, you must also remember that spiritual justice is taught in the words, "What you sow, ye shall also reap." The Law of Cause and Effect is activated in this vibration. The Law of Justice is also related to the Law of Karma as well as the Law of Retribution. The natural law requires that in time, all things must come into balance (Law of Balance) and harmony (Law of Harmony).

The Law of Justice blends with Law of Balance, Law of Equity and the Law of Moral Consequences.

> "Justice is the constant desire and effort to render to every man his due."
>
> ရ Justinian

> "Justice denied anywhere diminishes justice everywhere."
>
> ရ Martin Luther King, Jr.

> "An honest man nearly always thinks justly."
>
> ရ Rousseau

Law of Karma

[Aligns with Law of Cause & Effect,
Law of Compensation and the Law of Retribution]

Law of Life

The Law of Life gives expression and existence to everything; it is the manifestation of motion.

It is sometimes described in spiritual literature as the 'one law behind all laws'. That is, all other natural laws—both physical and spiritual— are simply different ways of expressing, operating, or manifesting through this Law of Life.

Will Durant said "Life is in its basis a mystery, a river flowing from an unseen source and in its development an infinite subtlety, too complex for thought much less utterance."

Today, humankind has entered a new dimension by investing time and study in the sciences. We have reached out into the heavens in search of more of the understanding of the mystery of life.

The Law of Life is the controlling force of the relationship between man and the Infinite source/power, or that which may be termed God. It is through your being, that you have the ability to adjust yourself to a higher vibration. This results in expressing the God power within your thoughts and actions. The Law of Life is, in essence, a controlling factor of your harmony or disharmony with nature, (the Source, the Infinite). Life is always in motion. The Law of Life is expressed in its fullness when you allow yourself to be in tune with the Infinite.

Why waste your life on doubts and fears? Exercise the power within you to do the work that is placed before you. You have the power of free will (Law of Free Will) to make the choices (Law of Choice) that will best edify you as well as your fellow man. Free will allows for a fullness of life.

Life has a purpose. You have come into the physical world as a unique individual with traits of your own. You have your talents, your strengths, and your weaknesses. Today, humankind is questioning why am I here and where am I going? You are in an age where humankind is not only being inquisitive about the world, but is seeking to find "the nature of its own being." Thoreau once said "On a sultry day on the sluggish waters of the pond, I almost cease to live and begin to be."

Meditation has become a popular topic of the day. The answers may be found in the stillness of the meditation process. It has opened the doorway to finding the answers through untapped knowledge. In humankind's search for the why of his being, many varied types of meditation are being utilized. This is good. Finding one's purpose of life, creates a service to humankind.

> "We are all in Life's great play—comedy and tragedy, smiles and tears, sunshine and shadow, summer and winter, and in time we take all parts...a 'good entrance' and a good 'exit' contribute strongly to the playing of a deserved worthy role."
>
> ❧ Ralph Waldo Emerson

> "Man loses his expression of life in matter—to find eternal life in the Light."
>
> ❧ Walter Russell

Law of Limitation

The Law of Limitation is the process of narrowing the mind by directing it to a specific arena.

The Law of Limitation is in action when you learn to set goals and eliminate excesses. Through the power of concentration, you can reject the irrelevant. You learn not to overdo because such action causes an imbalance. You must also be advised not to place limits upon yourself indiscreetly. If you do, you will definitely block the Law of Freedom from operating fully in your life. In order to allow these laws to function properly, as well as assist you in living in the flow of the river of life, it is imperative that you have a complete understanding of them.

Basically, the Law of Limitation is explained that by limiting your selection of goals, you will focus on those points that will assist you best in reaching your goal. You must review the overall situation. By understanding this law, you can transcend to that point termed individuality; that is, personality not only within, but demonstrated without. Once you have achieved an understanding and awareness, and relate to the divine within, limitation is no longer an issue. While the human will has limitations, the divine is unlimited.

> "Don't believe what your eyes are telling you, all they show is limitation. Look with your understanding, find out what you already know and you'll see the way to fly."
>
> ⁏ Anon

"You have powers you never dreamed of. You can do things you never thought you could do. There are no limitations in what you can do, except in your own mind."

                                  ℘ D. P. Kingsley

Law of Love

The Law of Love is the creative source and power of all life that lifts the heart and soul to the greatest heights of spiritual awareness.

What is love? There are many kinds of love. It can range from friendship to the supreme height where it is becomes pure service. Real love is the love of selflessness; the love that seeks nothing for itself and in its highest form embraces the whole of humanity.

This Law is extremely important! Because love is purifying, the realization of this law is the highest goal to be attained. It is through this law that the higher levels of consciousness are achieved. It is important to ask yourself, "How can I make this law function in my life so that it best serves me, as well as others?

The Law of Love allows the binding of the negative forces of hate, jealousy, pettiness, resentment, and revenge. The Law of Love provides you with freedom. This new found freedom allows you to pursue the positive goals of contentment, courage, harmony, peace, and tolerance—all of which bring balance into your life. By living in tune with this law, you can create a new and positive awareness for yourself as well as for others.

The love principle is the action of giving and its reaction of re-giving; it is the constructive force of all forces and it is the highest of vibrations. You demonstrate it when you place the needs and concerns of others before yourself. We can conclude the truth in the words that, "love is the voice of command, bringing the wayward atoms into harmony." It is true that love never faileth.

Let us ponder for a moment on the thought-provoking expressions of some noted teachers of the world on the subject of Love:

"The spectrum of love is patience, kindness, generosity, humility, courtesy, unselfishness, good temper, guilelessness and sincerity."

ဆ Henry Drummond

"There is a great power in the universe which has never been subject to the analytical scrutiny of laboratories, which cannot be resolved by chemicals or by scalpels, yet it is so real that it transcends all other forces which have been measured and weighted and dissected. It is the power of love."

ဆ Silver Birch

"The most essential part of a person's nature is his ruling love. It is this that shapes the whole character and constitutes, in fact, the individuality...everyone has his own love, or a love distinct from the love of another, and every one's own love remains with him after death."

ဆ Emanuel Swedenborg

"If you would have all the world love you, you must first love all the world."

ဆ Ralph Waldo Trine

"Love is the great solvent of all difficulties, all problems, and all misunderstandings. Apply love, by your inner attitude toward any human problem. Put aside the reasoning mind. Let divine love operate in and through you. Give from your inner self God's love, and you will be surprised to find that every problem will be solved; every knot loosened."

ℬ White Eagle

Law of Manifestation

The Law of Manifestation establishes that everything that is created was first a thought.

An idea in the mind of man manifests by creating its reality. It is through the unlimited creative power of the mind that progress results in our physical world. Applying this same concept in the spiritual atmosphere, you can manifest the experiences you desire. By using positive intent, it is a sure thing that your need or desire once sent out into the ethers will manifest accordingly. Always remember, you are co-creator with the Source.

The Law of Manifestation aligns with the Law of Allowing and the Law of Thought.

"Everything in the unconscious seeks outward manifestation and the personality too, desires to evolve out of its unconscious condition and to experience itself as a whole."

ℬ Carl G. Jung

Law of Mind

The Law of Mind provides that the higher mind has authority or direction over the lower mind. This in turn gives form and manifestation to all matter.

The Law of Mind dominates in your progressive (evolutionary) pattern. By totally using the power of concentration and in some cases, meditation, the lower mind can be brought into attunement with the higher mind. The dual capability of the mind reveals an objective and subjective mind or subconscious phase. Your objective mind relates to your external impressions and or conditions, while your subjective mind attunes you with the cosmic mind.

The Law of Mind has also been referred to as the Law of Subjective Attention. Dr. B. J. Fitzgerald in his book entitled *A New Text of Spiritual Philosophy and Religion,* teaches that "When relaxed in subjective mind, one has only to give concentrated inner attention to any person, place or condition and relevant thought—impressions may be gained immediately or in a matter of minutes. The inner mind is attuned to all knowledge within the universe. As we reach the higher heights of understanding, space and time are mental conditions. We can move in and through them at will. This is the foundation of astral projection and of all prophecy."

Dr. Fitzgerald also tells us "The subjective mind reasons inductively and not deductively as does the outer mind. This inner mind is controlled by suggestion and whatever premise it accepts, it sets to work to accomplish that premise with devastating power. It can build or destroy depending upon the controlling ideas which govern it. It will be controlled either by one's own thoughts, by the suggestions of other people, or by spirit influence; sometimes a combination of all three! The inner mind coordinates and directs all vital functions of the body. All forms of the psychic and mental healing depend upon this truth."

When using the power of your mind, you can redirect your life, your thoughts, and the flow of energy to meet your need on demand. Remember that wherever there is mind, there always is manifestation.

They are one. Control of your mind unfolds by using thought as its substance. Your mind is the storehouse of all thought. It is necessary to learn to control your mind in order to block any wrong thinking or other negative energy. The negative energies may generate chemicals that become destructive to the cells and organs of your physical body. This destructive force results in disease.

When the mind is activated and motivated properly, all manner of manifestation can be controlled. However, all inspiration, all wisdom, all truth, and all knowledge are dependent upon your capacity to receive the message.

> "We are shaped by our thought. We become what we think. When the mind is pure, joy follows like a shadow that never leaves us."
>
> හ Buddha

Law of Moral Consequences

[Aligns with the Law of Cause & Effect and the Law of Equity]

Law of Now

The Law of Now projects living in this precise moment.

The Now is the only moment you have; for yesterday is gone and tomorrow has not yet come. If you hold on to the negativity of the days gone by, you allow those negative factors to remain active, alive, and well. As a result, your feelings will react accordingly. When dwelling on the past, you are carrying old baggage along with you into the present. Many times, it is much too heavy and presents a difficult load to deal with today. If you are to move forward in your life, old baggage needs to be released and discarded forever.

If you dwell on the future or are anxious about tomorrow, your feelings react accordingly. You should understand that by living in the Now, issues such as high blood pressure may be avoided. Although in this earthly existence, it is wise to set a plan or goal for your future. However once set, you must return to living in the Now. It is the action you take at the precise moment that will lead to the next required action (Law of Sequence).

If you allow the memory of the sadness of yesterday (which was the Now then) to linger on, it interferes with your NOW. Life today can not be enjoyed when there is the interference of yesterday's negative vibrations. Likewise, the hurry to get to tomorrow or the imagined future (which will be the Now when it gets here), your present Now will not have been enjoyed.

At this very moment, it is necessary that you come into the understanding that all you have is "the here and now." It is at this very precious moment, that you do what is of essence in the here and now. If you accept that challenge, you will find yourself living in harmony and peace. Unfortunately in our earth life, the matter of man-made time seems to control our being. Remember that time doesn't really exist. What you know of as time is something that has been set by society by means of a tick-tock clock.

The present is the answer. Live for the moment! This does not mean you should not set goals or make plans. It does mean that those items should not take away the fullness of your present. They should not control nor fill your mind. The importance is to live in the Now and learn that no issue that is not of your present can affect you, unless you allow it to do so. For example, it does not matter if you have been treated right or wrong in the days gone by. If your mind revolves around the situation or the person of the past, you are resisting the Now. You are allowing the past Now to overtake your present Now, (this moment). At this very moment, drop all resentment of the past; it is old baggage. You are wise to forget the attack another person may have made on you. Let go of it! You need to stop and smell the roses of today.

"For many of us there are new discoveries to be made along the way; we are not our mind; we can find our way out of psychological pain; authentic human power is found by surrendering to the Now. ...These access points can all be used to bring us into the Now, the present moment where problems do not exist. It is here we find our joy and are able to embrace our true selves."

ε Eckhart Tolle

Law of One

The Law of One concludes that everything in nature is interrelated on some level of consciousness. Absolutely nothing, can stand alone.

There is only one Source and all else that is evolves from that source. Although there are individual entities, we must remember that all that is in being is a part of the One Source. The Law of One is the efficient reason of all things. The one law is absolute. It is beyond time, space and change. Every spiritual and physical law is encompassed within this law.

Every soul, whether incarnate or discarnate, is connected through the collective unconscious level; there is no break in the continuity of oneness. The Law of One manifests through each of us in varying degrees in our associations with each other. If you consider social circumstances, the Law of One reveals that your identity is just as important as what your relationship is to another.

> "Oneness of the Divine. It may be given a thousand names such as The Primary Cause/God/Energy/ 1. All that is created has itself, its Oneness."
>
> ℘ Sri Sathya Sai Baba

Law of Patience

The Law of Patience allows every action to have its own time, and its own season, in which to bring its action into fruition.

The Law stresses that there must be a desire or need and that you must nurture the expressed desire by taking a course of action. Once you do your part, then it is necessary to wait for the proper time for the desire or need to manifest. When patience is displayed, there is calmness and composure. Everything must function in its proper sequence (Law of Sequence) and timing (Law of Orderly Trend). Today, patience is often referred to as "staying power."

Many times, you may complain that your plan went astray. Just stop and take a moment to review that plan. Next, review how you altered that plan by taking another course of action in an attempt to speed up the process. You displayed impatience. It usually becomes quite clear that your intervention was the cause of things not happening as planned. Your impatience caused you to try and make things happen. If there is patience in all things, you will find that when they finally mature they do so to your best advantage.

"Life is all about timing—the unreachable becomes reachable, the unavailable becomes available, the unattainable... attainable. Have patience, wait it out. It's all about timing."

           ℘ Stacey Charter

Law of Peace

The Law of Peace identifies that calmness, serenity and tranquility must come from within.

Where there is harmony, there is peace. Peace comes in unity. Division that is harmful rather than beneficial leads to additional conflicts. Perhaps to bring about peaceful conditions, individually we must go into our chamber of silence and rest in our own quiet meditations. There we can grow inwardly by our solitude and prayer. If individually we achieve the state of peace, collectively we could change the world. The Law of Peace blends with the Law of Harmony and the Law of Unity.

"As human beings, we all want to be happy and free from misery...we have learned that the key to happiness is inner peace. The greatest obstacles to inner peace are disturbing emotions, such as anger, attachment, fear and suspicion, while love and compassion, and a sense of universal responsibility are the sources of peace and happiness."

           ℘ Dalai Lama

"Lord, make me an instrument of your peace; where there is hatred, let me sow love; where there is injury, pardon; where there is doubt, faith; where there is despair, hope; where there is darkness, light, and where there is sadness, joy."

           ℘ St. Francis of Assisi

Law of Personal Responsibility

The Law of Personal Responsibility states that although we are interrelated, each individual is accountable for his own conduct and obligations.

Throughout life, there is a constant reminder that you create your own happiness or unhappiness as you abide by the Laws of Nature (God/Source). Yes, unpleasant things may happen in your life; however, it is how you react that makes the difference. You are ultimately in control of your destiny. It is your responsibility to do what must be done in order to raise your level of consciousness. You can choose to be destructive or constructive based on your very own thought patterns and resulting actions.

Understanding brings growth. It requires that the negative patterns be eliminated. Error requires a price to be paid. On the other hand, you can create your desires; however, you must truly know yourself in order to fulfill them.

> "You must take personal responsibility. You cannot change the circumstances, the seasons, or the wind, but you can change yourself, that is something you have charge of."
>
> ∞ Jim Rohn

You are master of your fate. The key in functioning under this law is self-control. Experiencing your own valued nature, brings you closer to your potential (Law of Potential). It is up to you to realize your capabilities and the opportunities that present themselves. When the operation of this law is fully understood, you can do what you want to do as well as be whatever you choose to be.

There is no doubt that each must bear his own burden. It is your personal responsibility to make right choices that, in turn, help you create your own destiny. In this light, while you are free to choose and to obey or disobey nature's laws, you must also accept the consequences (Law of Cause and Effect). Your choices bring either reward or retribution.

> "One's philosophy is not best expressed in words; it is expressed in the choices one makes…and the choices we make are ultimately our responsibility."
>
>   ଚ Eleanor Roosevelt

Law of Potential

The Law of Potential states that the key for the achievements we can make in our life is within us.

Our spiritual essence is a creator. As you outline your desire, you also draw unto yourself all that is necessary to meet that goal. In your essential state you are pure consciousness. You hold a seed of uniqueness. No matter how another may try, they cannot be you, your being, actions or your thoughts. They may mimic you, but they cannot grasp the potential within you.

By the Law of Affinity, Law of Association and the Law of Attraction, you can draw unto yourself the circumstances needed to reach your goals. In like manner, you can also draw the people who can assist you in becoming successful.

In order to utilize this law to the fullest, the first necessary step is to follow the familiar teaching of Socrates—"Know Thyself and thou wilt know the Universe and the Gods." To meet your full potential, start from the inner and work outwardly. You are solely responsible for raising yourself to the highest level of being. This can only be accomplished by elimination of the negative and accentuating the positive.

Joel Goldsmith as well as many others in their numerous spiritual related writings, clearly encourages all of us to consistently enter into the silence and to have our daily meditations. You must first be controlled from within in order for you to properly control that which is around and about you. If you establish your desire clearly and utilize all of the creativity within you, as well as the possibilities that are around about you, it will result in a demonstration of your full potential.

> "Never underestimate the power of dreams and the influence of the human spirit. We are all the same in this notion: The potential for greatness lives in each one of us."
>
> ෩ W. Rudolph

> "A man who realizes the potential of his mind by means of introspection and contemplation, he does not lack self-confidence. He has control over his mind and he is able to realize its full potential."
>
> ෩ Sam Veda

Law of Prosperity

The Law of Prosperity is the condition of being successful or having plenty.

The universe sustains the well-being of humankind, both economically, socially and in health, and happiness. Prosperity abounds favorably. This law underlies the mental process that is a very important part in relationship to such laws as the Law of Abundance, Law of Desire, Law of Mind, Law of Spirit of Plenty, and Law of Thought. There is absolutely nothing impossible to anyone that has the will to control his life and surpass the norm. Jerry Gillis statement says it all—

"The strongest single factor in prosperity consciousness is self-esteem; believing you can do it, believing you deserve it, and believing you will get it."

This law blends well with the Law of Supply and the Law of the Spirit of Plenty. If negativity, lack, poverty, and self-limitation are accepted, they will without a doubt be yours. If on the other hand, you strongly refuse to accept these negative conditions, they will dissipate and no longer be a part of your consciousness. When you have the realization that you are a part of the Divine—a part of the total universe, you will also know that you rightfully deserve all that is available. You will prosper to the degree that you practice this law. At that point, the Law of Freedom is activated and all boundaries will disappear. Without boundaries, there is no limitation to the prosperity that can be enjoyed.

In order to live in a realization of prosperity, this law must be set in full motion. Keep hold of the thought of plenty. Those thoughts (Law of Thought), continually entering into the ethers will in turn bring about the condition of prosperity. Everything you need or desire will inevitably become reality.

Ralph Waldo Trine in his writing entitled, *In Tune with the Infinite*, 1897, stated that this law is better identified as "the Spirit of Infinite Plenty." If you recognize oneness with the Source of all things, it allows you to become like a magnet attracting (The Law of Attraction) a continual supply. The supply is equal to the demand. Use it wisely!

Visualize yourself in prosperous circumstances and then set your mind to work with the creative force of prosperity. Allow the magnet of the Law of Prosperity to work in your life. Know it! Believe it! Accept it!

The Law of Prosperity aligns with the of Law Abundance, Law of Spirit of Plenty, and the Law of Supply.

"A man is not rightly conditioned until he is a happy, healthy and prosperous being; and happiness, health and prosperity are the result of harmonious adjustment of the inner with the outer of man with his surroundings."

℘ James Allen

Law of Retaliation

[Aligns with the Law of Karma]

Law of Retribution

[Aligns with the Law of Compensation]

Law of Rhythm

The Law of Rhythm is a regular recurring motion functioning in alternating sequences.

The Law of Rhythm closely relates to the Law of Harmony. The Law of Rhythm embodies the understanding that in everything there is a measured motion—the constant flow of in and out or to and fro. This law is the underlying basis of the Law of Balance.

The Law of Rhythm is also closely related to the Law of Polarity. The Law of Rhythm is operating between the poles as a contrast of opposites. Since there is always action and reaction in some manner, it is necessary that it be harmonious. The grouping of the laws mentioned herein can be applied to many planes of existence.

The Law of Rhythm aligns with the Law of Balance, Law of Harmony and the Law of Polarity.

Law of Sequence

[Aligns with the Law of Cause & Effect]

Law of Service

The Law of Service legislates that we are all here to be of assistance to all of humankind.

The word service means "a contribution to humankind." What does the word serve mean? Webster writes that it is "...to be of assistance to or be a servant to another." In the evolutionary process of humankind, the importance of service is always stressed. Whatever service you can render, you can be assured that there is a need for it.

One can never become weary of this law. There is no greater joy than being of service to another human being. The Law of Service therefore very strongly relates back to "The Golden Rule."

The Law of Service requires you to learn your lessons of life. Being further fortified by the knowledge of Spirit, you can equip yourself for the tasks that are put before you. Then you should always pray, "...thy will be done." It is your duty to grow spiritually and become selfless, meaning you should consider others first. This is exactly why you are here on earth!

Simply stated, you are a servant of the unseen Spirit (God, the Infinite, and the Great Spirit). You are an instrument of the same Spirit. You should be willing and able to respond to any appeal. Service is given in bringing hope to the hopeless; bringing peace to the grieving, lifting up the spirit of the downhearted, bringing courage to the dejected, and replacing tears with laughter. It is through this service to others that the spark of divinity within you is expressed outwardly to others.

> "Life is not, we may say, for mere passing pleasure, but for the highest unfoldment that one can attain, to the noblest character that one can grow, and for the greatest service that one can render to all mankind."
>
>   ℅ Ralph Waldo Emerson

> "The greatest service we can do for another is help one to help one's self...And he who would be a leader of men must first be a servant of man."
>
>   ℅ Walter Russell

Law of Soul Evolution

The Law of Soul Evolution establishes a means of raising the self to a higher rate of vibration, resulting in a better state of being, thus becoming more spiritually elevated.

As you seek to improve, you must remove all fear from your emotional state and seek the higher truths. By learning life's lessons, your vibratory rate is uplifted. This creates a process of evolving into a higher level of consciousness. The advice given by Jean S. Bolen should be gladly accepted. She said "When you recover or discover something that nourishes your soul and brings joy, care enough about yourself to make room for it in your life." All too often, opportunity is afforded us but we tend to not find the time to make room for it. It is our choice that makes the difference.

The soul is ever in process of change. As you practice the Law of Love, it also assists in your soul's unfoldment. When you practice the Law of Service, it too aids in your soul's unfoldment. These processes allow you to move from a lower to higher and better state of being. It is the progressive development of organizational complexity. When you align your thoughts, emotions and actions with the higher self, you are filled with energy and enthusiasm. These factors result in a life that is in its fullness here and hereafter.

> "It matters not how strait the gate, how charged with punishment the scroll, I am the master of my fate: I am the Captain of my soul."
>
>   ∞ William E. Henley

> "He enjoys true leisure who has time to improve his soul's estate."
>
>   ∞ H. D. Thoreau

Law of Spirit of Plenty

[Aligns with the Law of Abundance,
Law of Prosperity and the Law of Supply]

Law of Spiritual Approach

The Law of Spiritual Approach represents the conscious act of an individual in creating its every thought that is then reflected in its words and deeds to reflect the power of being (God) within.

This capability resides only within the human being. Its approach can only be activated from within the being; perhaps by the conscience, or by the expressions of the heart. The utmost in the power of thought is expressed very commonly by word or by deed. When you learn to keep constant alignment with the spiritual approach, your higher self will be in full control of your life. Having mastered the spiritual, you will find yourself more closely in touch with the energized magnetic and power-currents of our vast universe. Carefully read, re-read and study the following quote and realize the fullness of the greatest gift given to humankind.

> "Man is the **only** unit in Creation who has conscious awareness of the Spirit within him and electrical awareness of dually conditioned light acting upon his senses. All other units of Creation have electrical awareness only. Man alone can be freed from the body to think with God, to talk with God and be inspired by His centering Light. All other units of Creation are limited in their actions to automatic reflexes from sensed memories built up through ages of sensing and recording such sensing as instinct."
>
> ಬಿ Walter Russell

Law of Subjective Attention

[Aligns with the Law of Mind]

Law of Substance

The Law of Substance states that all manifestations incorporate this essence, the thing itself—reality.

This Law of Substance is a basic underlying power of the Universe. It is the shadow behind all outward appearances or manifestations. It is known that everything in the universe is in a pattern of change for that is the only permanent condition.

Webster defines substantial as "actually existing; being the essential element; being real." He further states, that reality means "the state of being real, true, enduring, valid, fixed, permanent, and actual." An understanding of these definitions identifies that this law is an omnipotent, omnipresent agent. It is absolute and unchangeable. Nothing can confine it to boundaries. This oneness is Spirit. This source has been given many names; for example, God, Infinite Intelligence, Great Spirit, Mind, All, Allah, etc.

The Law of Substance blends with the Law of Substantial Reality.

"Everything that is, is of everything else that is. All things are indissolubly united."

&ro; Walter Russell

Law of Success

The Law of Success is the progressive realization of selected goals.

The Law of Success is the achieving of one's desires by setting out a plan and then working that plan. Hereward Carrington recorded in *Your Psychic Powers and How to Develop Them,* 1920, that there are three laws of success in order to achieve mental and spiritual success. They are as follows:

- ❖ "First: You must have in your own mind a clear conception of what you want.
- ❖ Second: You must make your thinking positive and not negative.
- ❖ Third: All your thinking must be constructive, that is, built about the goal or object you have in mind."

Many have become consciously aware of the fact that self-assurance, as well as an inner conviction is needed in order to succeed. Without a goal, a plan to reach that goal, and focusing on that goal, you certainly cannot expect to obtain your desire. Once again it brings to mind the idea of positive thinking (Law of Thought). Absolutely nothing can be achieved without it. Constructive thinking basically means that you must be consistent, and set your mind on that which you wish to achieve. You often hear the expression "go with the flow," but this is only effective if you are in a positive vibration.

Bessie Anderson, also known as Mrs. Arthur J. Stanley, said in a prize winning definition conducted by Brown Book Magazine in 1904, "He has achieved success who has lived well, laughed often, and loved much." The Law of Sucess aligns with the Law of Potential.

"The talent of success is nothing more than doing what you can do well, and doing well whatever you do without the thought of fame. If it comes at all, it will come because it is deserved, not because it is sought after."

                            ℘ Henry Wadsworth Longfellow

Law of Suggestion

The Law of Suggestion is the motive, or prompt by a mental thought shared orally that leads to another thought, action or creation.

When utilized in a very positive way this law brings success. Used in a negative fashion, it can cause distress. Suggestion will dispel suspicion and will summon cooperation. It provokes love and good work. Suggestion should always be constructive. It should call for advancement of all. Surely, you are quite familiar with making a suggestion to another. It may be as simple as offering another route to be taken, a simpler way of sewing a garment, or a quicker way of accomplishing a task.

In *The Law of Psychic Phenomena,* 1912, Thomas J. Hudson relates the understanding of what he terms "the subjective mind." Hudson gives "a glowing tribute to the responsiveness of the average man or woman to health-inducing suggestions vs. those of an injurious nature."

Your thoughts must always be clear in their intent. It is very necessary that you consider the importance of your thoughts (Law of Thought). You may consciously or unconsciously be telepathically sending a suggestion out into the ethers. The thought you send becomes deeply implanted in the subconscious of the receiver.

Today, in many establishments a "Suggestion Box" is provided for the employees and customers. Management reviews the suggestions offered and molds them in a way that can be best utilized to better their business. In order to win confidence in a product or promote business more effectively, major companies utilize various methods of soliciting suggestions.

You should carefully consider suggestions in preparing your daily affirmations. For instance, print a word or a specific statement on a white card in bold lettering, in color or black ink so that it is very distinct. Place it in front of you. Read it over and over again to help attain a certain result. An example might be, "I am happy, confident, and secure in my daily life" or "Every day in every way, my health is getting better and better!" This is in fact making a suggestion to your subconscious mind to advance your well-being. Reading the statement daily is the practice of visualization.

With the entrance of new thoughts in your mind, old thoughts are driven out. Therefore, a suggestion may be used to introduce a new thought that will bring new results. It should be clearly understood that you should only create suggestions verbally or in thought that you desire to see manifested in a positive way. Always remember, you will reap what you sow. It is the law!

Another example of suggestion may be considered in the art of healing. You can send powerful thoughts (suggestions) for the well-being of another. In this way, you can perform absent healing and be of service to humanity. Healing can be created by the transmittal of a suggestion that brings positive energy and revitalizes the physical and mental systems of another being. The power of suggestion has always been an important factor in the healing arena.

"Every thought is indeed a suggestion and a magnet, but all outward words and deeds are also suggestions, and they react upon ourselves and others to a far greater extent than we usually realize."

⋈ W. J. Colville

"In understanding the Law of Suggestion, you must realize that there are obstacles that are encountered for the beginners of this practice. The main obstacles are the lack of confidence and the lack of power of concentration. In order to successfully utilize this law, these obstacles must be overcome. Suggestions made only by appearance outwardly, produce shallow therefore transitory results, but suggestions due to interior force and strength of character, coupled with firm conviction and entire conscientiousness on the part of the suggestion, lead to permanent results."

⋈ Wilberforce J. Colville

Law of Supply

[Aligns with the Law of Abundance and the Law of Spirit of Plenty]

Law of Thought

The Law of Thought is the process of mental communication of an idea.

Thought is an incalculable energy force of the universe. It is said that thought is the cause and the effect is the resulting action. It encompasses and pervades all that is tangible to our senses here and hereafter. When transmitted silently, thought is often referred to as mental telepathy.

You must be attentive to your thoughts. It takes one thought to change your world within, as well as the world around you. By thought, your being and character are molded. By thought, problems are solved, creativity is enhanced and better ways for self and all of humankind result.

Higher vibrations result from positive and creative thoughts. Lower vibrations result from negative thoughts. A thought vibration established by a healthy active mind serves three functions—

* ❖ First: It determines whether the thought is constructive,
* ❖ Second: It determines whether the thought is destructive,
* ❖ Third: It determines the intensity of the thought as to negative and positive and the direction."

A very basic conclusion is that "Thought is the force underlying everything in the universe." Without a doubt, it means your every conscious act is preceded by a thought. Those thoughts that are dominating in nature, determine your dominating actions. Soon, your dominating actions become habits. And your habits result in your character.

Scientifically it is decreed that any thought that is entertained for a sufficient length of time will reach your brain, and without a doubt cause an action. The more a habit is demonstrated, it becomes easier and easier, until at some point no thought is required to commit the act. It is well to note that negative thoughts can and should be put out of your mind. You should never dwell on negativity. The process should be to substitute a new positive thought (subject) into your mind. This method should be used for removing any negative thought that enters your mind at any time.

It is said that thought is the parent of any act or deed. It is wise to remember that every thought you entertain is a force or power that goes out into the ethers. Thought once in the ethers comes back laden with its kind (Law of Affinity, Law of Attraction, Law of Cause & Effect and the Law of Correspondence). This is an immutable law. You shall attract to yourself from others as well as from the universe that which you create. It becomes very important that you do not allow thoughts to enter your inner world that you do not want to become a tangible thing in your physical world. It is a fact that by your thoughts you become a creator.

The Law of Thought aligns with the Law of Contradiction, Law of Excluded Middle and the Law of Identity.

"Create the best for yourself and for others. Every thought is a basis toward all progress or all retrogression, all success or all failure, that which is desirable or undesirable in our lives. It is the deep thinkers, the great thinkers and original thinkers who really move the world."

                                             ∽ Ralph W. Emerson

"Thought gives presence; love gives conjunction we bring into our presence or we go into the presence of whatever we fix our thoughts upon."

                                             ∽ E. Swedenborg

Law of Tolerance

The Law of Tolerance is the act of respecting the belief system of another individual.

Tolerance is recognizing that while another's belief system may be objectionable to your way of thinking, it is your duty to respect that person's freedom of choice (Law of Choice). The capability of doing this displays a demonstration of tolerance. When you are tolerant, you are allowing every individual whom you meet to follow the dictates of their own reason and conscience. However, while allowing other people to follow their own dictates, you may continue to hold the respective connotation you have about the issue.

Tolerance embraces fairness as well as an understanding toward the acts, views, and beliefs of your fellowman. Tolerance furthers communication which in turn relates to friendliness among peoples of the same or of different cultures. Once more the thought comes to mind, "Know Thyself". Next, it necessitates your being tolerant and allowing another to go on in their own path in their search of who they are as well as in their search for their Truth.

The Law of Tolerance aligns with the Law of Allowing and the Law of Freedom.

> "Freedom from prejudice—this encompasses neutralness in thinking, a willingness to allow the self to be led wherever Truth shall lead. Further, it demands an abandoning of any preconceived intolerances for these, like any closed area, do not permit the entrance of new concepts to enter into a person's consciousness."
>
> ∾ Helene A. Gerling

Law of Trust

The Law of Trust is the act or ability of relying on the thought or action of another individual.

The Law of Trust expresses complete confidence in another human being. Because of the previous behavior of an individual, you know how they will act as well as react in any situation that comes before them. You can be assured of whatever this individual represents—an expressed expectation. You may frequently hear an individual say that there is a mutual trust between him and his friend or between him and his business associate. This simply means they can totally rely on each other at all times and in all situations because they have previously fully demonstrated integrity in their character.

> "The answers to life's questions lie inside you. All you need to do is look, listen and trust."
>
>   ဢ Brian Tracy

Law of Truth

The Law of Truth is the comprehension of the knowledge of right thinking, acting, and living.

Truth does prevail! It is the Law of Truth driving us ever onward toward a higher awareness and a higher understanding. This practice furthers the advancement of our conscience. We should continually strive to know the truth of all things.

In *Ethics of the Great Jew* we read that: "Truth is the law of God. ...Truth means the realization of our being; and moral law means the law of our being. Truth is that by which things outside of us have existence. ...This absolute truth is indestructible. Being indestructible, it is eternal. Being eternal, it is self-existent. Being self-existent, it is Infinite.... It is transcendental and intelligent without being conscious...and because it is infinite and eternal, it fills all existence."

This law also teaches us correct understanding and it results in the demonstration of right thinking and action. It is a guiding law that tells us right from wrong. In fact, it might be closely linked to the conscience of man, (The Law of Conscience). Truth is a demonstration of growth into a higher understanding that will enable you to apply it in your every day life. Truth is not a thing that can be seen or perceived by the bodily senses; but truth is the essence with which an individual builds faith, hope and trust.

Truth is in a continual movement of upward development, reaching further to that which is reality. As you learn to know and project the truth, at all times, your consciousness is expanded. Therefore, Truth is constant; however, you may be constantly changing your concept of truth as you grow spiritually. Each day, you may become aware of more truths. As your understanding is raised to a higher degree, you become more elevated and you easily recognize and understand that what is a truth to you may not necessarily be a truth to another. Each is on his own pathway or pattern of truth (Law of Allowing and Law of Tolerance). You should always remain open to new understanding. You should be tolerant of others as they practice their truth.

Truth does not change, but you do become aware of truths that have always existed but had not yet come into your awareness. As you continue onward in your progression in life, you must be receptive to new truths as they present themselves. It is also true that in many instances man has made deductions based upon scientific discoveries. These deductions may have become his philosophies. They may or may not be truth.

"Truth is necessarily unalterable in character but our apprehension of it is necessarily progressive, though our knowledge of truth cannot alter, it does enlarge."

ହ W. J. Colville

Law of Unity

The Law of Unity is oneness; absolutely no separateness, and no division.

There can be no divisions because the universe is in divine order. Those things which may appear as separate or divisions to us, whether it is in persons, genders, polarities, or causes and effects, all blend into a oneness. Each little segment that one may recognize is an integrated part of the whole. The Law of One expounds on this subject.

The Law of Unity blends with the Law of One.

"He who experiences the unity of life sees his own Self in all beings, and all beings in his own Self, and looks on everything with an impartial eye.

ହ Buddha

Law of Use

The Law of Use can be expressed as having the possession of knowledge and its accompanied manifestation.

If you do not utilize the knowledge you have, it is similar to hoarding precious metals such as silver and gold. Understanding the expression of this law, brings awareness that a possession of knowledge if not put into action or service, becomes nothing but tinkling cymbals of brass—a vain and foolish thing. Knowledge, just like wealth, is intended to be utilized. What is the meaning of the term 'use? It is defined by Webster as "putting into action or service, or to carry out a purpose."

> "Use what talents you possess; the woods would be very silent if no birds sang there except those that sang best."
>
> ℘ Henry Van Dyke

Law of Vibration

The Law of Vibration states that all things seen and unseen in the universe exist in various rates and varying degrees of motion.

Vibration is the regularly recurring units of frequency in a given time frame. Although at times it may not appear so, everything in the universe is in a constant state of movement. We term that state vibration. Understanding of this law will allow every individual to be in control of self as well as their environment.

Vibration is energy in motion. Energy does not stand still, it is constantly moving. Since the rate of motion differs with each different type of matter, we have a variety of objects and forms in the universe. Thus, there is a difference between the various manifestations of energy, matter, mind, and Spirit resulting from the varying rates of vibration.

Every human being also has a rate of vibration and is able to raise that rate of vibration by attuning to a more refined state of consciousness or lowering it by attuning to negative vibrations. Positive or negative vibrations are created by your thoughts and actions. Change your mood and you change your vibration!

Spiritually speaking, the rate of vibration of the mind and soul can be changed by you. You can attempt and achieve attunement to a more refined state of awareness. In order to communicate with the world of Spirit, you must raise your rate of vibration to a higher and finer degree. This law is extremely important in the study of any phenomena. It can be labeled as the governing factor in communication between the physical world and the unseen world of Spirit.

Every vibration, sent out through the channel of thought, remains in the ether for all times to work as a negative or a positive factor. By bringing about perfect attunement to the higher rate of vibration, you can block all the negative vibrations. It becomes the task of every individual to determine just what vibration is desired within their own consciousness. This energy pattern is revealed in the individual's aura. The aura is explained as the electro-magnetic field surrounding the human body. This field moves from the surface of the skin of the human body outward into the ethers.

To continually evolve, it is imperative that you learn to control your thoughts, emotions, and actions. This control will provide a basis of understanding of man individually and collectively. It is through the Law of Vibration that you can attune to another. However, it must be recognized that what you will attract is the result of your own thoughts and actions. As you send, likewise you will receive.

Vibratory forces act as a sending and receiving station. What you send out into the ethers goes into the storehouse of all thoughts—the universal computer. This area might be described as the great sea of consciousness existing between the physical world and the World of Spirit.

Humankind can control the environment through the Law of Vibration as demonstrated in the area of thought. By the manner in which you think, you can create a positive or negative, or a productive or non-productive situation. These positive/negative thoughts influence all of us. The results of these thoughts are outwardly demonstrated in your actions and behavioral patterns. Emotion, desire, reason, and will, in fact any of the mental states, are accompanied by a vibration. When this is realized, you can understand that the correct statement is: "Thoughts create things."

"I am convinced that there are universal currents of Divine Thought vibrating the ether everywhere and that any who can feel these vibrations are inspired."

ಹಿ Richard Wagner

Law of Visible

[Aligns with the Law of Continuity]

The One Law operating in both the spiritual and physical was set in motion by God—the Infinite, the Source to govern all that has been created. This law is immutable and unchangeable.

The Spiritual Laws, or laws to live by, provide a way of life. It is your choice whether or not you desire to create a life of ease. The pathway of life provides for an opportunity of gaining more and more knowledge. Keep a journal and record your findings as you journey on the pathway of your personal life. The Spiritual Natural Laws listed herein were chosen because they are the laws-to-live-by and offer guidance as you continue on in your journey. The Laws are offered as a means of encouraging you to continue in your research— for life goes on.

Remember, that the natural law is continuously constructive, even when it appears by your lack of understanding to be destructive. It follows the pattern of need not just for today, but for the continuation and continuity of the universe. The natural law, no matter at what level, is harmonious.

Our universe is a universe governed by natural law resulting in an orderly trend. Humankind may have social lawlessness on earth, but there is a higher power—a universal law that governs manifestations of every kind.

Although at this time miracles are looked upon as a variance from the law, we cannot close our eyes to the fact that this may somehow be possible. Perhaps, there is a law not yet understood in our level of consciousness or being. However, at humankind's present level of understanding, miracles are a theory and cannot be justified. Up until this moment, no one has ever witnessed the natural law set aside for any reason, for any person, nor by any plea. However, the current understanding may be changed at a future date by a revelation of new knowledge. As we continually grow in knowledge and truth, we must leave the doorway open to receive more truth.

In order to insure your own continued evolution, you must come into a full understanding of both the spiritual and physical laws. As you come into an understanding of a law, it is then required that you put that law into practice in your daily life. In time, you will have an understanding of all of the laws and become in tune with the Infinite. Then, it is your task to "teach them by showing them."

Shakespeare's familiar words ring true, "There is nothing new under the sun." It is just a matter of understanding of the law. As you continue in your research and study, you will come into a clearer understanding of that law. Then, the unseen source will encourage you to experience the divine power within yourself.

As you continue in growth and understanding, an ideal motto might be:

"I do not believe today exactly what I believed yesterday, and I hope I do not believe tomorrow exactly what I believe today; for I want to progress in every twenty-four hours."

ဆ Marylyn J. Awtry

VI.

THIRTY-FIVE

PHYSICAL NATURAL LAWS

T HERE ARE MANY, many physical and scientific laws that govern our universe as well as the spiritual laws. In order to come into a more comprehensive understanding of natural law, we must become familiar with the physical laws as well as the Spiritual laws.

The Spiritual Laws provide a way of life for the continued growth of our soul and our character. The Physical Laws provide for the continuity of the operation of our physical world. It must be clearly understood that both the Spiritual and Physical are but one law. One could not operate in perfect accord without the other.

All branches of human endeavor are governed by natural law. The selected laws given below are termed physical natural laws. They apply more directly to our physical world and existence. Some of the laws also apply to our spiritual well-being.

It is necessary to understand that there is an overlapping of the spiritual and physical laws in many areas. The Physical Laws have been accepted in the world of science. These laws are universal; simple, but absolute and true. They have never changed since they first came into the awareness of humankind. They are considered to be eternal laws. As we understand it today, everything in the universe must comply with the laws of the universe. To date, we have found no exception to any of the natural laws.

There are many natural physical laws. At this time, the laws most common to your daily living have been selected to be brought into your awareness. An understanding of these laws, will give you a better comprehension of humankind's place in the scheme of things.

The Natural Physical Laws

Law of Acceleration

The Law of Acceleration is demonstrated in the field of Biology and in the field of Physics.

In the field of Biology, it explains that the order of development of a structure, or of an organ is directly related to its importance to the main organism.

In the field of Physics, the meaning is that the rate of change of velocity is either in magnitude or direction. Whenever there is any change in velocity, no matter in what direction, it is termed acceleration. For example, every time we change the velocity or speed of our automobile, we are in effect operating within the Law of Acceleration.

Another explanation is that the acceleration of an object as produced by a net force is directly proportional to the magnitude of the net force, in the same direction as the net force, and inversely proportional to the mass of the object. Sir Oliver Lodge wrote

"Acceleration is the effect of a single or resultant force acting upon a particle of matter, and its value is the ratio of the strength of the force to the mass of matter moved. This is known as Newton's Second Law of Motion."

Law of Action and Reaction

The Law of Action and Reaction states that for every force there is an equal and opposite force or reaction. This is also known as Newton's Third Law of Motion. The Law of Action and Reaction is a statement in Dynamics.

Let us suppose you have your study book placed on a table in front of you. The weight of the study book is the force which acts downward. Since the book does not move by itself, there must be some equal, but opposite force acting on it. This force is exerted by the table top for it is exerting an upward force. Thus, we have two forces in action. The book is exerting a downward force and the table top an upward force. This is a simple example of two forces that are equal yet opposite.

Force results from interaction. Forces are always in pairs. For every action, there is an equal (in size) and opposite (in direction) reaction force. The Law of Action and Reaction aligns with the Law of Motion.

Law of Adhesion & Cohesion

The Law of Adhesion and Cohesion unites or holds together the atoms of being in all forms of matter.

Adhesion considered separately is the act or state of being united or attached. Unlike cohesion, adhesion is the force of attraction between the particles of the bodies of a different nature.

In the science of Physics, the term cohesion means the state or force which keeps in contact with particles of bodies of the same nature. This makes them form a continuous mass. Thus, we can conclude that the distinction is made that an adhesive force which acts to hold separate bodies together and a cohesive force, which acts to hold the like and unlike atoms, ions, or molecules of a single body.

Law of Alchemy

The Law of Alchemy expresses that everything is always in a changing condition, except for the indestructibility of energy and its changing forms.

Alchemy began as an ancient art of obscure origin that sought to transform base metals (e.g., lead) into silver and gold; it is the forerunner of the Science of Chemistry.

As an individual, you have the ability to create changes in any conditions that come before you. You can take situations which appear to be negative and reflect on them as challenges to help you grow. This natural law operates in both the physical and spiritual realms. The Law of Alchemy aligns with the Law of Change.

Law of All-or-None

The Law of All-or-None states that a nerve impulse resulting from a weak stimulus is just as strong as a nerve impulse resulting from a strong stimulus.

It is explained that a weak stimulus cannot produce a strong stimulus since it can only produce its strength of weakness in like manner and vice versa. It must be all of one and none of the other.

Law of Attraction & Repulsion

The Law of Attraction states that creations of like vibrations tend to be attracted to each other by a chemical affinity. The Law of Repulsion states that the same vibrations may tend to repel or withdraw from each other by a chemical affinity.

The Law of Attraction and Repulsion are usually discussed jointly. We previously studied that the Law of Attraction provides for the unity or affinity of atoms or objects in both the animate and inanimate kingdoms. The magnetic power of a being attracts other objects of like affinity (Law of Attraction). Perhaps, vibratory forces act as the signal for magnetic action. However, the same variance in vibratory force can signal an act of repelling (Law of Repulsion) or withdrawing. This permits bodies to recede or drift further away from each other. Once again, we find this law is interacted upon by other of the natural laws such as The Law of Thought—"As a man thinketh" and the Law of Desire—"as a man wants."

In a determination to eliminate all negativity, the result will bring you into a realization of the Law of Positivity. Therefore, when you realize and understand the interaction of all of these laws, you must recognize that you attract and or repel by your own thoughts as well as by your behavior.

T. T. Hilarion relates to the law in regard to Spirit by stating that "The Law of Attraction is the demonstration of the power of Spirit while the Law of Repulsion governs the form. Spirit attracts Spirit throughout the greater cycle. In lesser cycles, Spirit temporarily attracts matter. The tendency of Spirit is to merge and blend with Spirit. Form repulses form and thus brings about separation. During the great cycle of evolution—when the third factor of Mind comes in and when the point of balance is the goal, the cyclic display of the interaction between Spirit and form is seen. The result is the ordered cycles of human beings, the planets, beings, and that of an atom."

Law of Biogenesis

The Law of Biogenesis reveals that life comes only from life. The Law of Biogenesis is known as Huxley's Fundamental Law.

Life cannot suddenly spring into existence from nothing. The result of nothing is nothing. Anything that is produced must come from something. Life must originate from life. "Bios" means natural life with cells and germs. All life must spring from a source. Biogenesis is the Law of Life for all degrees of life.

The Law of Boyle & Mariotte

The Law of Boyle & Mariotte states that the volume of dry gas varies inversely with the pressure exerted upon it provided the temperature remains the same.

Robert Boyle was a British scientist/physicist who was born in 1627 and passed to higher life in 1691. He was the very first scientist to conduct tests on what he called the "springiness of air." After numerous experiments, he formulated what has been termed as Boyle's Law.

Law of Causation or Causality

The Law of Causation or Causality states that every change in nature is produced by a cause and has an effect.

This principle recognizes the fact that cause must always precede any effect. Causation is the agency that produces an effect while causality is the regularly correlated events of phenomena. The Law of Causation and Causality are principles in Philosophy. Therefore, the Law of Causation or Causality aligns with the Law of Cause & Effect.

Law of Conservation of Energy & Matter

It has become recognized that matter and energy are not separate and distinct, but they are definitely related to each other. The Law of Conservation of Energy & Matter further states that energy cannot be created or destroyed but it can change form. The Law of Conservation of Energy and Matter is a principle in Physics.

Consequently, considering the laws of Conservation of Energy and Conservation of Matter requires they be combined into one encompassing Law. This combination of law concludes that matter and energy are interchangeable. The fact that energy and matter are neither created nor destroyed substantiates that the total amount of energy and matter in the universe is constant—there is neither more nor less. It simply continues.

In "*Man and the Universe*," 1908, Sir Oliver Lodge states that "Energy expended by a body which does work is gained by the body upon which the work is done; so that energy is neither gained nor lost on the whole; it is constant in total quantity and is amply transferred from one body to another without increase or decrease."

The conversion of one type of matter into another is always accompanied by the conversion of one form of energy into another. It is understood that many transformations of energy do not involve chemical change. However, it is also clear that all energy involved in any change at all always appears in some form after the change is completed.

In *"Man and the Universe,"* Sir Oliver Lodge explained that "The atoms of matter were once believed to be indivisible; now, however it is supposed that some of them at least can resolve themselves into other atoms, and these perhaps into electrons but the ultimate units are still assumed to be constant in number and indestructible."

Law of Constant Proportion

The Law of Constant Proportion states that every definite pure substance always contains the same elements in the same proportions and weight. This Law of Constant Proportion is a statement in Chemistry.

For example, every drop of hydrogen peroxide has the same proportion of hydrogen as well as the same proportion of oxygen. It weighs the same as every other drop of hydrogen peroxide. Therefore, there is a harmonious relationship of parts to each other or to the whole.

Law of Contraction & Expansion

The Law of Contraction and Expansion is a principle of continual change of intermolecular spaces.

The word contract is defined as "a reduction in size" while the word expands is defined as "an increase in size." This operating force in turn causes a change in the vibrational force.

Law of Contradiction

The Law of Contradiction states that a thing cannot at the same time both be and not be of a specified kind. The Law of Contradiction is a principle in Logic.

For example, an object cannot be a chair and not a chair at the same time. Something cannot be hot and cold at the same time; it is either hot or it is cold. Something cannot be wet or dry at the same time; it is either wet or it is dry. An object can only be one thing at a time; it either is or it isn't.

Law of Cycles

[Aligns with the Law of Evolution]

Law of Diminishing Returns

The Law of Diminishing Returns states that at any given stage of technological advancement, an increase in the productive factors applied beyond a certain point fail to bring about a proportional increase in production. The Law of Diminishing Returns is a principle of Economics.

In other words, after a certain point of production has been reached, no matter how we try and no matter how much the effort, the return on the effort no longer equals the amount of work put into it.

Law of Effect

The Law of Effect expresses that in the method of trial and error learning that the satisfying or successful behavior is always repeated. It establishes that unsatisfactory or unsuccessful behavior is not repeated. The Law of Effect is a statement in Psychology. This law is known as Thorndike's Law of Effect.

In further study of this law it becomes apparent that under normal circumstances, as we learn by trial and error, we tend to automatically reject patterns of behavior that we do not find rewarding or self-satisfying.

Law of Energy—Active, Static or Kinetic

The Law of Energy is power and is manifested in its ability to effect motion. This is a Law of Thermodynamics.

Active Energy

It manifests through electronic attraction, expansion, contraction, heat, light, electricity, etc. Since we know everything of substance (physical matter or substance unseen) is subjected to constant change, we know that energy and motion are always in action.

Static Energy/Potential Energy

This is simply energy in a stationary condition producing a state appearing to be at rest or stalled and awaiting a purposeful situation in order for it to be released. Potential energy is considered to be stored energy that is able to do the work, if it were released.

Kinetic Energy

This is a situation of a form of matter being attracted or being repelled. The kinetic energy moves in the direction of whatever the directing force may be.

Law of Evidence

The Law of Evidence states that none but mathematical proof is susceptible of that high degree of evidence called demonstration that excludes all possibility of error. The Law of Evidence is also known as Taylor's Law.

In the investigation of matters of fact, such evidence cannot be obtained. The most that can be expressed is that there is no reasonable doubt concerning them. Therefore the true question in trials of fact is not whether it is possible that the testimony may be false, but whether there is sufficient probability of its truth; that is whether the facts are providing satisfactory evidence.

Competent evidence is that which the law requires as fit and appropriate proof in the particular case. Satisfactory evidence may be termed sufficient evidence. Evidence that satisfies an unprejudiced mind beyond a reasonable doubt is considered to be sufficient evidence.

Law of Evolution

The Law of Evolution guarantees a constant, unfolding of progression in all of nature. It can clearly be described as the things within being expressed outwardly. It is a gradual assumption of new appearance or degrees of appearances.

Periodicity means a state of occurring as recurring at fixed intervals in time. A writer once stated "all events tend to move in cyclic trends in constant circular movement of continuous recurrence." For example, civilizations rise and fall, nations rise, flourish and decline and yet others start their rise. History reveals that governments are rising and falling and another is rising. This law is also observed in philosophical thought, religious guidelines, scientific theories, and fashions—the new becomes old, and the old becomes new.

This law basically deals with the effect of each state of consciousness upon each individualized being. It teaches that each spirit, in or out of the physical, should seek to become self-reliant.

The evolutionary process is basically the foundation for all law. It should increase man's understanding of his purpose in being. Man is on the earth plane to grow physically and spiritually—to evolve—and this is what is guaranteed by The Law of Evolution. Growth! However, the rate of that growth depends on the conscious awareness of the individual being. Often, it is a slow process; however, it continues on purely by persistence.

Huxley expressed his understanding by saying "Evolution or development is at present employed in biology as a general name for the history of the steps by which any living being has acquired morphological and physiological characters which distinguish it."

The Law of Evolution has been regarded as a scientific law; however, it must also be recognized as a spiritual law. Man in his process of growth should be constantly reaching out for higher understanding as well as gaining a greater awareness. The Law of Evolution perfectly aligns with the Laws of Cycles and Periodicity.

Law of Excluded Middle

The Law of Excluded Middle states that if one of two contradictory statements is denied, then others must be affirmed. The Law of Excluded Middle is a principle in Logic.

An example of this law can be explained by stating that if two statements are being discussed with exactly opposite view points, and if we decide or prove that one is false, the other one must automatically be true.

Law of Gender

The Law of Gender states that there is a gender manifested in everything—masculine and feminine principles are always present and active.

In the Hermetic teachings, the masculine principle has always been considered positive (strong) and the feminine principle seen as negative (weak). All of Creation is subject to this law. We find it is effective on every plane of causation. It operates in the avenues of generation, regeneration, and creation. The operation of the law of Gender on the plane of energy produces varied phenomena of light, magnetism, electricity, attraction, repulsion, and many other similar phenomena.

Gender, though not so termed, is also a part of the mental phase. In 1893, Thomas J. Hudson in his book entitled *The Law of Psychic Phenomena,* advanced his theory of objective and subjective minds. He explained they were found in every individual. Others have termed it conscious and subconscious or voluntary and involuntary, active or passive. While it may be different terminology, the underlying principle is the duality of the mind. Therefore, the conclusive understanding is that the male and female gender is manifested throughout the universe.

Law of Gravity

The Law of Gravity states that any particle in the universe attracts any other particle with a force that is proportional to the product of the masses of the two particles, and inversely proportional to the square of the distance between them. The Law of Gravity is a statement in Physics.

There is a more familiar practical approach to the law of gravitation. The force of gravity exerted by the earth is the force which causes bodies to fall downward. It is this force that keeps everything from flying off the face of the earth. It is also the force by which we measure to determine the weight of an object. This law is indeed a law essential to our orderly physical existence. Without it, life as we know it would cease to exist.

Law of Impaction

The Law of Impaction is the transmission of action from one plane to another.

This law utilizes the inner principles of polarity. It is the act of bringing a force of a subtler plane through a denser plane. It is the act of advancing a force in evolution by developing "form" aspect. This law is based upon the Law of Attraction of the center.

Law of the Jungle

The Law of the Jungle dictates survival by any means possible. It is presumed to be in effect among animals in their natural state. The Law of the Jungle is basically a code.

The Law of the Jungle is also presumed to be in effect among people who are unrestrained by an established law, whether they be civilized, personal, or civic control.

Law of Least Effort

The Law of Least Effort states that the things of nature's intelligence function with effortless ease, carefree, and harmoniously.

In the least action, there is the least resistance. It aligns with principle of harmony and love. For example, in nature the grass just grows; the tree just sheds its leaves and blossoms with new leaves every spring. This free energy can be applied to anything. Love is also an example of an effortless function that can operate spontaneously. When motivated by love, we expend no additional energy.

The three components of the Law of Least Effort are:

1. Acceptance: The universe is just as it should be.
2. Responsibility: We cannot blame anyone but ourselves for our present situations. The challenges in life are seeds of opportunity and serve to promote our evolutionary process.
3. Defenselessness: There is no need to convince or persuade others of our point of view.

This reminds us to look to the Spiritual Laws of Allowing, Detachment and Now. It is best to always be in the present—the

"Now." Once we have learned to accept these factors, we are then practicing the Law of Allowing and life will flow effortlessly.

As recent as the June 2005 issue of *Cognitive Psychology*, it stated that "It has been found that the Law of Least Effort may apply to the human brain." In the article, the latest scientific research at Carnegie Mellon University has discovered how the brain solves a problem. The results indicate that "There are partially separate networks within the human brain which support language and visual-spatial processing. They suggest that our brain may seek to minimize the mental workload by choosing the strategy that makes less work for the brain. The brain may use the method less costly for the individual by selecting the one in which he or she is most efficient." These recent studies further attest to the value of The Law of Least Effort.

Law of Motion

The Law of Motion states: "A body at rest remains at rest and a body in motion remains in uniform motion in a straight line unless acted upon by an external force." The statement has been recorded as Newton's First Law of motion. This is a statement in Dynamics.

For example, you reach your destination and park your car on of the street. Once parked, the car will remain their indefinitely as long as it is not touched. Now, let us suppose your parked car is bumped into by another moving car. What happens next? Your car will start to move and then will gradually come to a full stop. This is a demonstration of Newton's First Law of Motion.

The car that bumped into your parked car was an outside force that moved your car. Then, another outside force termed friction caused your parked car that had been forced into motion to stop. The law expresses that if there had been no friction to act as an outside force, your bumped car would have kept on moving forever. The Law of Motions aligns with the Laws of Action and the Law of Reaction.

Law of Opposites

The Law of Opposites is universally expressed in male and female—thesis and antithesis.

Webster describes the word as "things that are in sharp contrast to one another" or going one step further "elements that are so far apart as to be totally irreconcilable." It is in the knowledge of this law, that we find the great magical secret of regeneration which is essentially identical with transmutation.

Law of Orderly Trend

The Law of Orderly Trend states it is under the cooperation of which order is universally made manifest from the groupings of atoms in the formation of the minutest organism, to the arrangement of the planetary bodies in the constitution of gigantic Solar Systems.

It makes known that there is a regular sequence and orderly procession of all of the phenomena in the universe. It is recognized if given a certain cause, there will most definitely be a certain effect. This law once again makes the emphatic point that there is no such thing as chance within the universe. From the smallest to the largest, everything operates in a systematic fashion (Law of Sequence). We also recognize that for every effect, there is a cause. The Law of Orderly Trends aligns with the Law of Divine Order.

Law of Periodicity

[Aligns with the Law of Evolution]

Law of Polarity

The Law of Polarity states that, particular properties of a body or substance in nature tend to reside in specific places termed poles.

This law relates to the fact that every thing is dual; everything has its pair of opposites. The only difference is the degree of a higher or lower vibration. For instance, there is upper and lower, shorter and taller, wider and narrower, faster and slower, hotter and colder, bitter and sweeter, hate and love, active or inactive, masculine or feminine, etc. When we consider these factors, it can be said that the poles are negative or positive in nature.

The word Polarity is derived from the Greek word 'pole' which means "one of two points in which the axis of revolution of the earth cuts the surface." As such, polarity refers not only to possession of two poles, but variation in properties so that in one direction they are opposite of what they are in the other direction.

The phenomenon of The Law of Polarity is generally considered to be brought about by the Law of Attraction. The polarity of our planetary system is manifested by the relationship of the sun to the planets. The planets orbit in perfect harmony to each other. Nature also provides manifestation of the law in the natural principle of sex differentiation. An Ancient Occult axiom is:

"Everything has its opposite, that is the other pole of its manifestation."

Law of Reflection

The Law of Reflection is the turning back of light from a specific surface. The Law of Reflection is a statement in Optics.

The word reflection means "the act of throwing back a form or image." When light falls upon a plane surface, it is so reflected that the angle of reflection is equal to the angle of incidence (the occurrence or frequency of the occurrence). The incident ray, reflected ray, and normal ray, all lie in the plane of incidence.

In layman's terms, reflection is the turning back of light from a specific surface. However, how much light is reflected, depends upon three things:

1. The kind of material that we are attempting to reflect light off of,
2. How well the surface of that material is polished, and
3. The angle at which the light strikes the surface of the object.

One very common and familiar example, is the reflection reproduced in a mirror.

Law of Resistance

The Law of Resistance states it is a retarding force acting upon a body from the outside and actively opposing any propelling force.

This may also be an active pull back exerted by some other agent. If we understand the word resist, it means to simply fend off or to attempt to offset an action. Dick Sutphen in his book *Lighting the Light Within,* 1987, stated "Resistance is fear...this law of resistance assures that you let go of fear by encountering it until you are forced to deal with it by learning detachment (Law of Detachment)."

Law of Sufficient Reason

The Law of Sufficient Reason states that there is logic in everything; there is a definite reason why it should be as it is, rather than be otherwise. The Law of Sufficient Reason is a principle in Logic.

For instance, a dog barks; therefore, it is sufficient reason to say that it can not be a cat. A cat meows; therefore, it is sufficient reason to say it can not be a dog.

Law of Synchronicity

The Law of Synchronicity is expressed as being in the right place at the right time. It can also be said to be simultaneous or happening or existing at the exact same moment.

Synchronicity was explained by Carl Jung as being on the same order of causality. Everything flows harmoniously within the universe when in a balanced expression. Everything is then in divine order.

Law of Vibration

The Law of Vibration states that there is a regularly recurring unit of frequency in any given thing, whether it is animate or inanimate. This rate of vibration determines its very nature.

The term vibration can be expressed as an oscillation or movement by a rhythm or pulsation. When the vibration of an inanimate object is changed, its nature is changed. Water forms into ice and gases form into vapor and steam. While we are aware of the rainbow of color, our physical eye cannot adapt to finer vibrations (invisible to the eye) and produce other color; however, it is there. Likewise, we are aware that many animals are attuned to a rate of vibration of sound not heard by the human ear.

Science has proven that everything in the universe is in a continuous state of motion; and, has termed it as a frequency or a rate of vibration. It further states that all that is termed matter and energy are but modes of vibratory motion.

"All manifestation of thought, emotion, reason, will or desire, or any mental state or condition, are accompanied by vibrations, a portion of which are thrown off and which tend to affect the minds of other persons by induction. It is this principle that produces the phenomena of telepathy."

80 Hermetic Teaching

There are many more physical laws of the universe. The above examples of Natural Physical Laws are just a few selected from the many because they are the laws most commonly known to most of us. Some of these physical laws give us an example of the proximity of physical and spiritual laws, and in many cases their overlapping capability.

Everyday of your life, somewhere, somehow, another law will be introduced to you. It is not a new law; it just has come into your awareness. Everyday as you purposefully seek knowledge and understanding, you will become aware that the study of Natural Law is on-going in nature. It justifies being termed "The River of Life."

While you just concluded reading these selected laws of the spiritual and the physical, in reality you have just begun your journey into your new life of going with the flow—simply by living the natural laws.

As you read the words written by Kenyon Jones in *God's World*, allow yourself to come into a harmonious attunement to his expression of truth. Although these words were written 1919, or ninety-one years ago, they are very appropriate today. Truth remains constant.

"We are living under God's law. We came into life in accordance with that law and in harmony with it we shall depart from this life. But that does not make us less important than the material things around and about us. They are never lost. They may change—they may enter into new combinations—but to the finest division of matter, nothing is ever lost. Life and nature are related. Everything that exists is related because it all emanates from God (the Infinite)...between the cradle and the grave, we work out certain fragments of our progress.

If the Source (God, The Infinite, the Power) had never opened the door, had never broken the seal between earth life and spirit life, then upon theory and logic we would be obliged to make our conclusions. But the seal was first broken by putting into every soul certain Godly instincts.

There has always been that inner knowledge that life does persist. The great fundamental Law of Life reaches us in the flesh the same as it does in the Spirit. We are Spirit now as much as we shall ever be—living merely under different conditions. But, our thought and sense of being are the things of the Spirit. The Law that pertains to the living in one place and under one group of conditions also pertains to the Spirit anywhere and under all conditions."

If you practice living in tune with the natural law, you will be living in the flow of the river of life. That in itself, makes for an easing of conditions in your life. Since you now know that stepping out of alignment (cause) with the natural law produces negative results (effect), you can change your life by living the law. It will bring peace to your soul. It will bring joy into your life.

By allowing a more in depth understanding to reside within your own capacity of being, and allowing more knowledge to flood your consciousness, may you continue to evolve and achieve an expanded awareness every day—and then, even then, the search continues—for life goes on!

Allow your life to become one of ease, create that joy and peace of mind, simply by slowly entering into the meandering stream of understanding…until it flows like the River of Life!

VII.

SEVEN NATURAL LAWS

FOR UNFOLDMENT

And the Four Hidden Keys

W E ALL ARE born with innate abilities. The Universe offers everyone the opportunity for personal growth—both physically and spiritually. Whether or not you accept the opportunity of making use of your innate abilities, is simply a matter of your own choice.

Edgar Cayce, The Sleeping Prophet, said "You are born with a soul and psychic abilities are a soul quality and each soul is endowed by its Maker with choice, with that birthright." In essence, it is a gift that has been freely given to every soul. Whatever you do with your gift depends solely on your own desires as well as the choices you make in this lifetime. You will gradually grow from one stage of life into another physically; and, you will also grow or stagnate spiritually. What is your choice? Will you go through life analyzing every step of the way? Will you allow yourself to follow the knowing within you? The decision is yours to make. What will you choose to do?

The soul qualities Cayce speaks about are termed "Extra-sensory Perception (ESP)" and "Intuition." It is "a knowing" within you. The human faculties transcend the limits of current human knowledge. In many instances, due to the lack of understanding, we fail to use our greatest gift of Intuition or the sixth sense of Extra-sensory Perception (ESP). In *Contemporary Definitions of Psychic Phenomena and Related Subjects* by SAM, Inc., the definitions related to the subject are given as follows:

> **"Intuition** is a faculty or ability of the human mind to know or be aware of knowledge that has not been obtained through reasoning, inference, or awareness of currently known facts."

> **"Extra-sensory perception** is an experience of spontaneous awareness to conditions of an object, a state of being, influence or event without contact with a known source; occurs without a conscious awareness of people or persons involved therein."

Every stage of your life offers you another opportunity to come into greater awareness of universal knowledge. Opportunity is at your beck and call. Every stage of awareness increases the capabilities and power of your conscious and subconscious mind. An understanding of the natural laws and how they affect your life can assist you in deliberately creating your successful future. If you have the proper intent, the unfolding of your innate abilities will enable you to enhance your life both here and hereafter.

The awareness of the vibratory rate around you relates directly to the level that you have unfolded your psychic skills. Your desire should be to unfold your innate abilities to the level that will allow you to have the ability to alter your consciousness at will.

Every two thousand years, we enter a new age. Very often, we begin to feel the effects of the change of the age several years before its entry. At the turn of the century, we welcomed the entry of the Age of Aquarius. The Age of Aquarius is characteristic of change as well as a time of blending. That changing and blending can be reflected in a shift in our moods, our actions and intentions. Some will adapt easily, while others will struggle with the new energies on the horizon. It is also the arrival of spiritual enlightenment—an awakening! Intellectually, the influence will be mystical, scientific/inventive, and religious. It is a time when humankind will go within for the needed answers.

The Rosicrucian Order makes this very appropriate statement in regard to the Age of Aquarius in this statement—"The Aquarian Age will see the blending of religion and science to such a degree that a religious science and a scientific religion will be formed—each respecting and learning from the findings of the other and it will promote health, happiness, and enjoyment of life. …Science and Altruism will rule during the Aquarian Age." The Order continues by accurately stating that "Since Aquarius is an airy, scientific, and intellectual sign, it is a foregone conclusion that the religion of that Age must be rooted in reason and able to solve the riddle of life and death in a manner that will satisfy both the mind and the religious instinct. In this respect, the Western Wisdom is preparing the way for the Aquarian Age by breaking down the fear of death engendered by the uncertainty surrounding the post-mortem existence. These teachings show that life and consciousness continue under Laws as immutable as God, which tend to raise man to increasingly higher, nobler, and loftier states of spirituality."

The hidden things of the mind have now evolved from the laboratories of the 20th Century and are becoming known to the multitude in the 21ˢᵗ Century. Little by little, more and more, demonstrations of the inner being of humankind are becoming recognized as natural faculties. Psychic ability can no longer be hidden in the darkness of a closet. It can no longer be practiced in secret. Your innate faculties are becoming a very active part in the river of life in the 21ˢᵗ Century.

Without a doubt, many times intuition has made a breakthrough in your life; however, just as many times it has probably been suppressed or simply ignored by you. It may have been looked upon as a silly idea or just a thought going through your mind. Sometimes, it has been suppressed simply out of fear of the unknown. Why is that the case? One reason is simply because the seat of the psychic faculty within has eluded humankind for such a long, long time. Throughout the ages, humankind has searched for knowledge everywhere. They sought answers to the Who, What and Why of their being. However, in most instances, they failed to find answers because they failed to look within. Another reason may be that intuition was considered an uncommon trait. It appeared to be reserved for fortune tellers and the like. Now, the Age of Aquarius has arrived! It has ushered in a raise in the vibratory rate of spirituality. This increased rate of vibration opens the doorway to those precious gifts buried deeply within your soul—your psychic self.

It is very clear that you go about your daily life with the five physical senses being a given. You do not stop to think about seeing, hearing, tasting, touching, and feeling. They are natural senses to you. Your programmed mind, where your beliefs are stored, is at the subconscious level. The time has arrived to allow the intuitional mind to break out of its confinement and become helpful to you. The intuitional mind is more powerful than your programmed mind because it is the knowing from within. It is understood that our brain is divided into a left and right hemisphere. Each sphere has its delegated purposes. The main differences appear to be that left brain is logical, analytical or rational in thinking and the right brain is intuitive, creative, visual, holistic and synthesizing. Since the intuitive mind is in the right brain hemisphere, it produces creativity which results from the basic level of a capability from within. It is the producer of all great inventions of the ages. Stop a moment and review in your mind the great scientists of the centuries. They not only used their intuition but they had also trained their intuitive mind to function magnificently. As a result of their inventions, life became easier for the multitude.

You may sometimes find that the message in your mind will come spontaneously. You can make it more available to yourself by giving more attention to intuition and extra-sensory perception. Why overwork the reasoning mind when you have a capability that you can use in addition to it? Learning to pay attention to this knowing that is within you, increases your ability to become more consciously aware of it all—it is a storehouse of knowledge. It is a more reliable source because it is connected to the universal mind. In the chapters that follow, you will be given guidelines in learning how to develop your innate abilities.

Just think, if you will harness the intuitive capability within yourself, this inner knowing will give you peace and comfort as well as the advantage of being "in the know." It will give you a great advantage over others as they hold on only to reason. It will enable you to see things you have never seen before. You might even say it will change your perception of things. Self-awareness and a way of seeing or knowing in greater depth are being recognized as a somewhat common trait. It becomes clear that awareness and intuition are compatible and really are inseparable. Once you learn to trust your intuition, you will find it becomes more prominent in your life and is a constant, truthful guide and director. Once you learn to use your intuition, you may find that many new opportunities are introduced to you. It is very possible that things you never dreamed of will become available to you.

Opportunity

Opportunity has been defined as "a time or occasion that is suitable for a certain purpose; favorable combination of circumstances, or an uncertain event with a positive probable consequence." The consequence can be negative or you can take the initiative to make it positive and profitable for yourself.

Sometimes, opportunity may come as an obstacle placed in your pathway and you must struggle through that obstacle. Other times, it seems the way just opens up for you to walk right on through, over, or around the obstacle without any particular effort on your part. Although opportunity is another gift of life, it very often evades us. However, opportunities continue to be unlimited.

You may often question, why is this happening to me? It has been frequently said that obstacles in your life are some of the tests of life. For what are you being tested? Who is doing the testing? Have you passed the test? Dwelling on the 'why' of it all, is just wasting away precious time. Do you remember what you have learned about the natural law? The statement was made earlier, "It is not what happens to you that matters, but rather how you respond to what happens to you." What you allow, will become your reality! So instead of brooding over any given moment for which you have no answer, why not just turn it into a positive opportunity? How? Follow the dictates of the natural law and of your intuition. It will work for you every time! It will never fail you!

"Opportunities do not come with their values stamped upon them. Everyone must be challenged. A day dawns, quite like other days; in it a single hour comes, quite like other hours; but in that day and in that hour the chance of a lifetime faces us. To face every opportunity of life thoughtfully and ask its meaning bravely and earnestly, is the only way to meet the supreme opportunities when they come, whether open-faced or disguised."

&) Maltbie Babcock

How Do I Know?

It is only natural that your next question would be, "How do I know I have intuition or the sixth sense of extra-sensory perception"? The answer is varied. Foremost, the faculties of intuition or extra-sensory perception demonstrate activity of the mind, or it can be said to be a demonstration of mind-power. Everyone will acknowledge the fact they have a mind. It is natural, therefore, that you have all the faculties of the mind.

Other ways of answering this question may be: You may just simply know. You may have a sudden flash of knowing! You may have an all encompassing knowing, without a wisp of a doubt. You may have an extremely strong impression. You may hear a voice as a whisper or it may be loud and clear. You may see a vision. It may come in a dream state. It may be as simple as saying you have a hunch or a gut feeling. No matter how it comes to you, it is the most wondrous blessing! When the gift makes itself known, accept it! It is at that very moment that the door has opened. It is suggested you gladly enter in. Learn to go with the flow and enjoy your new found experience of life.

Some people may ask the question "Is not this against the teachings of the Holy Bible?" The answer is "Emphatically not"! The Bible teaches about the spiritual body, healing, physical manifestations, dreams and visions, speaking in the unknown tongue, speaking through trumpets, independent voice, materializations, trance, direct Spirit writing, levitation, ministry of angels, and more. Following all the Sages preceding him, one of the Master Teachers, Jesus the Christ, demonstrated the natural law many times throughout his short ministry. It mattered not whether he was in the towns, on the hillsides, or upon the troubled waters. The multitudes witnessed numerous demonstrations but yet they continued to question his capabilities. Jesus, responded to them very clearly, saying:

> "Most assuredly, I say to you, he who believes in Me, the works that I do he will do also; and greater works than these he will do... ."
>
> ℂ John 14:12 KJV

In 1ˢᵗ Corinthians, Chapter 12, the Apostle Paul instructs us further on the Gifts of the Spirit. He tells us "But the manifestation of the Spirit is given to each one for the profit of all: for to one is given the word of wisdom through the Spirit; to another the word of knowledge through the same Spirit; to another faith by the same Spirit, to another gifts of healing by the same Spirit; to another the working of miracles, to another prophecy, to another discerning of Spirits, to another different kinds of tongues, to another interpretation of tongues. But one and the same Spirit works with all these things, distributing to each one individually as He wills."

Most certainly, Paul would not have mentioned the gifts in such depth if they were of little or no value to us. The unfolding of the gifts will improve your life as well as allow you to be of greater service to others. Your inner growth will determine in what manner you live, as well as to what degree you have evolved spiritually. However, it is to be remembered that it is your choice whether or not you accept the gift that has been so freely given. Only that, which you allow, can become productive in your life.

The Natural Law Is The River Of Life

The key to living a life of pleasure, ease, and reward is by making it a practice to live in accordance with the natural laws every day. Learn to use the power of your psychic self (soul) and trust your own intuitiveness. This capability is the continued process of unfoldment of your innate being, your spirit/soul. Now you may ask, "How can I allow the laws to be beneficial in my life"? It is very necessary that you learn to mould your character in accordance with the highest teachings. This will establish a firm foundation upon which you can build. In doing so, your soul growth continues on in its process that started long before physical birth.

There are some people who have given very little thought to their soul. They know they have a soul and they have heard that the soul is eternal. They have heard of heaven and hell, but it stops short right there. Entertaining the idea of elevating their soul's awareness has never entered their conscious mind. Then, there are others who even classify the whole idea as ludicrous.

It is very important that you raise the vibration of your soul now while you are on earth plane and experiencing earth's lessons. As you strive to raise your consciousness, you will become more and more aware of the key that opens the doorway to your psychic self (soul). This innate part of your being offers you guidance in your journey here as well as hereafter. It is like a subtle stream flowing gently until it becomes one with the river.

Once you have accepted the fact that the natural laws are the laws to live by, another question comes to mind—"Which of the natural laws apply particularly to the unfoldment of my soul and which of the laws apply to my innate abilities?" The answer to the question is simply that while many of the laws interact with each other, there are seven of the natural laws that apply most directly to the unfoldment of your soul and of your soul-sensing capabilities. The seven laws are listed as a guideline to follow as you proceed in the process of your unfoldment.

The Seven Laws

No. 1. Law of Soul Evolution

The very first of the Natural Laws to be considered is the Law of Soul Evolution. It is necessary that you raise your state of consciousness to the higher levels (the Cause), if you expect your desire to manifest (the Effect). Do you recall the words of Jean S. Bolen's quote? She said "Whenever you recover or discover something that nourishes your soul and brings joy, care enough about yourself to make room for it in your life." The soul is subjective and takes the thought of the conscious mind and diligently acts upon it. The soul only carries out the orders you present to it. It should be your desire to give it the most direct and best orders at all times. It should also be your desire to live in a balanced vibration of harmony at all times.

The first step in evolution of the soul is the practice of eliminating all negativity from your life. In order to be able to receive the higher truths of the universe, you will want to remove all obstacles that are blocking your pathway in life. The process of accomplishing removal of the stumbling blocks includes but is not limited to: fears, negative thinking, and all negative practices. Make a list of all negative-action terminology in your vocabulary, such as: No, I can't, I won't, I fear, I hate. Think a few minutes to be sure you have included every word or phrase that is applicable to you. Slowly, read them over just one time and then burn them to ashes and bury them. Emphatically state: "Out of my consciousness, out of my world!" Now, on a 3 x 5 card, make a list of positive-action terminology, such as: Yes, I can, I will, I love. Again, include all words or phrases that are applicable to you. Put the card in a place it where you can see it and read it daily.

The next step for you to consider is the avoidance of negative behavior; such as: suspicion, gossip, slander, worry, jealousy and demonstrations of ignorance. These traits are not conducive to the evolvement of your soul. Think on this subject for a moment. Now, make a list of all of your behavior practices that are negative. Slowly, read them over just one time and then burn them to ashes and bury them. Emphatically state: "Out of my consciousness, out of my world!" Now, on a 3 x 5 card, make a list of positive factors, such as: courage, faith, generosity, hope, justice, love, and reasonableness. Train yourself to be cooperative **with** others and to be tolerant **of** others. Master the Law of Use. Be orderly in all things and learn to use your time and energy wisely. Be reasonable and strive to have balance in all that you do. Balance is one of the prominent laws of nature. Above all, be yourself. Never try to imitate anyone.

You should desire to attain the highest vibrations possible in order to activate your soul in striving to become 'all knowing'. Read uplifting literature. Appendix "A," provides a list of several recommended books on the subject of soul growth. Be selective and associate with evolved individuals. Always, strive to be kind and patient. Practice the Law of Love in your life at all times. Allow the Law of Association and the Law of Attraction to function for your highest good by being the best as well as by doing your best. By cultivating these positive factors, you will draw a higher rate of vibration into your consciousness. This will assist in elevating your soul qualities. This behavior will result in attracting the best. Only that which the inner you reflects, can the outer world experience.

Before going on to Law No. 2, it is suggested you go back and reread the Law of Affinity, Law of Attraction, Law of Association, Law of Balance, Law of Cause and Effect, Law of Harmony, Law of Love.

No. 2. The Law of Personal Responsibility

What does responsibility mean? Webster states "Responsibility is being able to answer for one's conduct and obligations; able to choose between right and wrong; trustworthy...to be responsible; anyone person can assume a responsibility for something." Webster further states that "Personal responsibility relates to an individual's character, conduct, motives; the qualities of a person." Based on the definitions of these two single words, it would be correct to say that "Personal Responsibility is the obligation and liability of an individual in relationship to one's own character and conduct."

The Law of Personal Responsibility is an important factor in proceeding in the unfoldment of your soul—your psychic self. Once you accept the responsibility for your deeds, good or bad, you are bringing yourself into alignment with your soul's purpose. It has been said before and it is being said again, "You are master of your fate and captain of your soul!" You are creating your tomorrows and the cause that you deliberately create, will give you the just effect. Cayce said:

"Every soul should become a channel for the universal consciousness and to express that consciousness in his relationships with his fellow man. The highest spiritual ideal must be made a vital and living part of the experience."

Your thoughts are creating change and initiating different vibrations into motion in your life. You must remain in full control of your thoughts at all times. All wrong thinking and wrong doing must be eliminated before growth can transpire. As you grow, your mind is continuously expanding and your personal responsibility necessitates that you nurture your mind and soul accordingly. This mind expansion creates various rates of vibration that affect your continued growth. No thought is ever lost in the sea of consciousness of this universe. Whatever you send out into the ethers is returned unto you ten fold. It is without a doubt, that you are accountable for every thought and action that takes place in your life. Constantly be aware that your thoughts do create your tomorrows.

Are you ready to step up to the plate and accept your personal responsibility for your thoughts and your actions? Once you are ready and willing do so, you will have taken one giant leap in the pathway of raising your consciousness, and in the opening of your intuitive awareness. Individually, we are responsible for our personal soul growth and collectively we are responsible for the welfare of the world in which we move, act and have our being. As you grow in this pathway of awareness, you take on the responsibility of making every day the best day in your life and in the lives of others.

Before going on to Law No. 3, it is suggested you go back and reread the Law of Allowing, Law of Choice, Law of Example, Law of Karma.

No. 3. The Law of Awareness

The Law of Awareness is the next step to be considered in the unfolding of your soul growth and your intuitiveness. It is the gateway to success. As you venture forth, you will see clearly that self-awareness is one key opening the door to your spiritual growth. It can also affect your personal growth. In order to grow in any aspect, you must be aware of all things relating to that particular aspect. Webster's definition states "Awareness is perception or knowledge; to be cognizant or conscious of." Actually, awareness is the recognition of that which is and always was but is now known because you have opened your mind as well as your eyes to that great sea of consciousness. Awareness is simply a "knowing or realization." The word conscious by itself relates to a mental awareness. Every step of the way provides an avenue for growing into a full awareness of who you are and the fullness of your potential. Once you have aligned yourself with the reality of your true self, knowing yourself, and trusting yourself, you can then expand your awareness to include all that comes within your vibration in your day-to-day activities.

In your journey through this lifetime on earth, you should desire to remain open to all avenues of learning. Knowledge and wisdom are two more keys to living life more abundantly. You can study and become more knowledgeable; however, someone once said something to the effect 'to acquire wisdom, one must observe.' That is a fact. Allow your eyes to bring everything around you into your conscious world. You can only deal effectively with that which you know and understand. Without a full knowledge of a situation avails you to the possibility in making an error in judgment. Being open, allows you to experience new conditions and situations. It gives you the opportunity to study new fields of endeavor. Within you, is the inherent power to expand your consciousness beyond your present state of awareness.

Everything that comes into your awareness assists you in becoming a better person. It is necessary to pay attention to those thought waves that sweep through your mind. Allow those inner feelings to become one with you. Once your intuitive nature is expanded, it allows for a greater perception of everything. Your intuitive nature is limitless. Once you begin to trust your intuition, life becomes easier. Be aware that intuition is not a substitute for reason, but it has been said that all reason tends to act on the information brought to it through the gateway of intuition. Intuition has always been inspirational but you must seek to achieve it. By becoming fully aware of yourself and all that surrounds you will result in successful experiences of intuition.

Before going on to Law No. 4, it is suggested you go back and reread the Law of Awareness, Law of Conscience, Law of Personal Responsibility, Law of Soul Evolution and the Law of Truth.

No. 4. The Law of Attraction

The Law of Attraction suggests that the creations of like vibrations or attunement tend to be drawn to each other by a chemical affinity. Positive or negative vibrations sent out into atmosphere return to the sender in like manner. Negative breeds negatives but positive breeds positives. If you are to enrich your soul and your innate abilities, you must always be aware of what you are attracting unto yourself. It is very necessary that you understand that your thoughts and behavior are the attracting energy. That which you allow, becomes of utmost importance.

It becomes extremely important that you understand that you are a co-creator of your life. Your every thought has a powerful magnetic capability of attraction. In this physical life, it is paramount that you attract those of high intent. In order to attract those from the Spirit side of life who have raised their consciousness to greater heights, you must dedicate yourself to working on raising your own personal vibration. You must become consciously aware of your thoughts and your actions every moment of every day. You will attract that which you are mentally—thoughts create things. Your life's desire can become reality by the understanding and practicing of this law. There is no need to spend your hard earned money seeking to buy some special magical gimmick to bring your dreams into reality. They do not work anyway! All that is necessary, is for you to practice the simple process of the Law of Attraction and create your desire. Energy expended by you in a positive manner, will draw like energies unto you. It is up to you to create happiness, health, wealth and a special kind of life, simply by keeping your inner being attuned to the power of the this law. It is very necessary to remember that in order to apply this law effectively, all negativity must be removed from your consciousness.

If you continue to consider expanding your world of the paranormal, you will find that in every branch of psychic investigation this Law is predominant. It is wise to remember that the Law of Attraction brings like vibrations into perfect attunement and harmony. It relates back to what you sow, you shall also reap.

Before going on to Law No. 5, it is suggested you go back and reread the Law of Balance, Law of Cause & Effect, Law of Free Will, and the Law of Thought.

No. 5. The Law of Desire

The Law of Desire will assist in creating the causes and the effects in your life. This law governs how you think and how you act. Your first step must be to dismiss that which you do not want as a part of your life. Remove all negativity from your thoughts and actions. As you move into the understanding of your psychic self, it is necessary that you have a complete awareness of that which is around you—seen and unseen, as well as a full comprehension of the Law of Attraction.

Once you establish a desire, you must then concentrate on that specific issue. By concentrating, you can draw all thought or focus to the condition or situation which will allow the desired results to manifest. You must know clearly and specifically exactly what you desire. Your expectations of what will unfold must be in exact agreement with your desire. The mind must be focused in one direction. If you work in harmony with the law, it will always result in manifesting your desire.

You will never receive anything beyond the height of your own desire. You must have a burning desire to receive the manifestation. The quality of your desire underlies this process. There is no need to wonder how or when your desires will be fulfilled. It simply happens, because life runs in an orderly sequence (Law of Orderly Trend and Law of Sequence) and the result is the fulfillment of your desires.

Before going on to Law No. 6, it is suggested you go back and reread the Law of Awareness, Law of Choice, Law of Creation, Law of Intention.

No. 6. The Law of Thought

Having read the previous pages, you are now aware that by your thoughts and resultant actions you attract to your own being an inanimate control over your material and spiritual conditions. If you desire the best, you must think and act in a manner both physically, mentally and spiritually to attract the best. Without a doubt, if you think in a negative manner, those thoughts will create unsatisfactory conditions in your life. The result will compound and bring unhappiness; however, negative conditions can be changed by substituting a positive thought vibration. The more you study the topic of Thought it becomes quite obvious that it is necessary for you to learn how to control your thoughts. Previously, Ralph Waldo Trine was quoted as saying "A thought can be put out of the mind easier and more successfully, not by dwelling upon it, not by attempting to put it out directly, but by throwing the mind on to some other object by putting some other object of thought into the mind." This is one method of thought control.

Every moment of every day, you think. Without a doubt, you are creating your tomorrows. When you are having thoughts, you will find they produce feelings about things. Considering all that you feel, results in the way you behave or react at any given time. By your thoughts, you are also forming habits in your life. It has been said, 'actions speak louder than words.'

Thought is a condition created by the mind. Every thought remains an idea until it is given energy and put in motion. Be extremely careful what you think, for it is the creator within you expressing itself. Your thought (the cause) will give you the result (the effect). Your thought creates your behavioral patterns and results in cause and effect in your life. Remember that all thought remains in the ethers for all time. Therefore, your thoughts may be received by other minds that are attuned to the same rate of vibration. Be very careful what you think!

Another step to be considered in your unfoldment is that by your thought, you will create the atmosphere for your failure or for your success. Your thoughts must project a sincere desire, supported by a sincere intent and surrounded with the light of integrity. Thought is the parent to the act. It is wise to remember that the underlying force of everything is thought. It is a proven fact that every conscious act you commit is preceded by a thought.

In your busy world of today, you are not always aware that a great deal of time is given to your outer world. In most cases, you do not experience enough quiet time—the time where you can evolve your inner, spiritual self as well as your thought-life and power. Perhaps, it would be wise to recommend that you enter the silence at the close of every day. Review your thoughts of the day. Then, cancel those thoughts that have not or will not be productive in your life. Substitute new thoughts. Quiet time will allow you to be in tune with the Infinite. In turn, it results in aligning yourself with your powerful thought capability.

Before going on to Law No. 7, it is suggested you go back and reread the Law of Intention, Law of Manifestation, Law of Mind, Law of Success and the Law of Thought.

No. 7. The Law of Vibration

As you think and as you act, you are creating various degrees of motion. The rate of this motion is understood as the Law of Vibration. Vibration always expresses itself through the two great channels of force and matter. Every force that exists, both visible and invisible, maintains a rate of vibration. Every animate or inanimate object has its own rate of vibration. The rate of vibration dictates the form or state of being that they assume.

In *Contemporary Definitions of Psychic Phenomena and Related Subjects* by SAM, Inc., it states:

> "**Vibration** is the regularly recurring units of frequency in a given time frame; periodic motion forced from a state of balance; a current or emanation that may be sensed by a medium or psychic."

Peggy Barnes, a knowledgeable teacher in days gone by, expressed her thought on the subject in this manner:

> "Every vibration sent out through the channel of thought remains in the ether for all time, working for good or evil, dependent upon the nature of the thoughts."

Your aspirations and desires grow from your present conditions and circumstances. Your positive aspirations and desires will activate the necessary vibrations conducive for your growth. You will draw to you vibrations of the same rate and of the same quality that you project (Law of Attraction). If you desire attunement with the most elevated teachers here, as well as in the Spirit world, it is necessary to raise your rate of your vibration. How do you do that? You must build, preserve and protect your own magnetic centers and energies. It is required that you maintain the highest thought vibrations. The transmitter of all thought is a particular vibration that carries the thought into the vast sea of consciousness. That vast sea is termed "ethers." Whoever attunes to those thoughts in the great sea of consciousness is affected by either the negative or positive current of the thoughts you set in motion.

The next area to be considered is living your daily life in the most positive condition, followed by the practice of prayer, listening to soft peaceful music, and basking in dedicated quiet time, known as meditation. In addition to these soul growth factors, it is wise to always display positive, energetic vibrations in your daily behavior. Each of these practices can be of assistance to you in achieving your goal. If you want the best in your life, you must create the best by entertaining positive vibrations. Your understanding of the workings of the vibratory forces and raising your rate of vibration is of little value unless activated and put into positive use.

Many of the Spiritual Natural Laws influence the innate abilities of humankind. The fine tuning of your innate abilities results in your application of the seven interrelated laws. It should be reflected as well, that it is most difficult to mention one law without another requiring an expression in some degree. Your soul evolution is dependent upon your mastering the natural laws. The hidden keys are Intent, Consistency, Persistence, and Patience. Once you have reached that goal, the Law of Vibration can bring about the desired results of the demonstration of your innate ability. The next question is, Are you a medium or a psychic, or both?

VIII.

MEDIUM, PSYCHIC OR BOTH

THE TERMS MEDIUM and psychic are often confused, misinterpreted, or used synonymously. Clarification of these terms will establish the foundation for formulating a correct understanding. The booklet by SAM, Inc. entitled *Contemporary Definitions of Psychic Phenomena and Related Subjects*, states

> "A **Medium** is an apparent sensitive who communicates with and obtains knowledge from discarnate beings; the two classes of mediumship are: mental—use of the mind and mental processes; physical—producing phenomena that involve material or material-like manifestations, such as levitation, etc."

> "A **Psychic** as a noun is synonymous with the term sensitive; as an adjective, it describes the paranormal character of abilities and events occurring outside the known physical laws and principles."

Is there really a difference between a person being identified as a Medium and a person being identified as a Psychic? Absolutely! Understanding of the terms medium and psychic as shown above, clearly establish that a Psychic is not a Medium; however, a Medium may have the additional faculties required to also be classified as having psychic ability.

The impressions received by a Psychic are received from a source outside the known physical laws and principles. In general, the term psychic is used to describe anyone who may be able to give information pertaining to the past, present, and the future. Although the source outside the known physical laws and principles from which the information is gleaned is unknown, the data given may still be extremely accurate. Again, you ask, "So what is the difference?"

The difference is clearly that a Medium's main objective is to **"prove the continuity of life."** This adequately differentiates a Medium from a Psychic. A Medium has the capability of communicating with those who have left the earth life and continue to live in the Spirit World. Basically, there is no death and there are no dead. Physical death is just a shedding of the physical shell and assuming a change of consciousness that allows the soul to continue moving into a new dimension of life. This new dimension is termed the Spirit World. A Medium's purpose is **not** to tell the past, present or future. The main and **most valuable** quality of Mediumship is the ability of **spanning the bridge between the earth plane and the Spirit World.** By attuning to the Spirit side of life and communicating with those in that dimension, the continuity of life becomes a proven fact! In order to demonstrate this communication, a Medium is required.

It is evident from the demonstration of mediumship, that every Medium works differently. Some Mediums may be able to provide a description of the Spirit when that spirit lived on earth, give their name or nick name, or give other detailed facts about the Spirit's earth life. The Medium may bring a message from the Spirit entity. Other impressions or messages received by a Medium, may be from a source outside of the known physical laws and thus allows a medium to also act in the capacity of a Psychic. Every medium has unfolded this ability to whatever degree is possible for that individual.

The two classifications of Mediumship are expressed as Mental and Physical. There is a wide range of phenomena that falls under these two classifications.

How Can I Become a Medium or a Psychic?

There are many roads that lead to the unfoldment of your innate abilities. Every individual must choose the avenue with which they feel most comfortable. However, no matter which road you choose, be aware of the fact that there are absolutely no short cuts in the process! While many ninety-day wonders have appeared now and then, they have also rapidly disappeared. Sincerity, intent and dedication are mandatory in order to unfold your abilities properly. Appendix "A" provides a listing of several books that recommend various methods of unfoldment.

The guidelines presented herein are offered as some of the basics to encourage you to investigate the many avenues of unfoldment that are available to you. My goal is to stimulate your desire to unfold your innate soul-sensing, whether that is as a psychic or as a medium. Remember, your innate abilities were a gift at birth. However, it is your responsibility to actively unfold and utilize that gift. Immediately you think, well how do I get started on this journey? Since it is imperative that you always seek spiritual upliftment before stepping into the unknown, the previous chapters have covered how to raise your consciousness; how to come in tune with the infinite; and, how to live in the flow. Now, let's take the next step of the journey.

The Journey

Before you begin any journey, you have to know where you are going in order to determine how you are going to get there. You need a plan of action. The very first thing I suggest is that you purchase a ruled journal; it can be a bound book or a loose-leaf binder. On the very first page, write your name and the current date. In this journal, you are going to record your road map to success. You should keep your journal readily available in order to document all that takes place on your own personal journey. You should make an entry in your journal after ever session. You should also record any unusual happenings along the way. You should record every change in method, or date as well.

To help you gather your thoughts, think on these questions.

- ❖ What do I want to accomplish on this journey?
- ❖ What is my intent?
- ❖ What is my proposed start date?
- ❖ What is my proposed finish date? How and why can this date be modified?
- ❖ What would I hope to unfold?
  - ☐ Psychic   ☐ Medium   ☐ Healer
- ❖ Why do I want to have success in this journey?
- ❖ What do you know about the innate abilities?
- ❖ Which books will I read for soul growth?
- ❖ Which books will I read for unfoldment of my innate abilities?
- ❖ Where will I seek other like minded people?

After thinking about each of the ten items, write your answers in your journal. You have now taken another step and are on your way in your own journey.

Goal & Intent

What is your goal? Your goal is one of the cornerstones or the foundation upon which you are going to build. Your goal should be to unfold the innate capability within yourself to the best of your ability. At this point, you do not know just what capability you may have within. Time will tell. Do you desire to be a medium and speak to those on the other side of life, seek psychic unfoldment with the ability of seeing the past, present and future, obtain the gift of healing, or perhaps become an inspirational writer? While you may have a desire in mind, it is very possible that your ability will unfold in a different area. Are you willing to accept whatever unfolds? You must understand that no matter which road you may choose, strict discipline and control of yourself is absolutely required.

What is your intent? Repeated again is the fact that in order to unfold any of the gifts, you must first have a burning desire. You must have a sincere intent as your second cornerstone of your foundation. What do you want to achieve? Why? There is nothing at all that can prevent you from having success, except yourself. The next step should be mastering the ability to allow your mind to be free. Persistent and consistent practice will give you the results needed to continue in the unfoldment process. How can you learn to set your mind free? In answer to that question, Joel Goldsmith in *The Thunder of Silence* gave us four keys. He said "You must have

1. Sincere intent, and be
2. Consistent,
3. Persistent, and
4. Patient.

Are you ready to do whatever it takes?

IX.

MECHANICS OF UNFOLDMENT

Step 1 – Basic Mechanics

The Conditions

SELECT A COOL and quiet place where you will not be disturbed.

Select a convenient time for every day. You may choose early in the morning. However, you may find you are pressured knowing that you must leave for work at a certain time. Early morning, may not be conducive to a good session for you. Perhaps, you may choose late evening only to find that you are too tired. Select the best time frame for yourself. If you must change the time schedule, go with your inner feelings. In your journal, enter all the time and date changes that were necessary.

Next, decide upon the length of your sessions to be devoted to the practice. You may find it necessary to decrease or increase the allotted time. Enter all changes in your journal.

Do you wish to have soft music, candle light or incense? Again, go with your inner feeling and if it is not right for you, change it. Enter all changes in your journal.

- ❖ Dress comfortably. Loose clothing is suggested.
- ❖ Select a comfortable sitting position.
- ❖ Always eat lightly before a session.
- ❖ Never practice if you are over tired.
- ❖ Have a dimmed lighting in the room.

Step 2 – The Arts

The Art of Breathing

Breathing is a normal faculty. When you were born, it took a simple jolt by the doctor and you began to breathe on your own. Throughout your lifetime, you have never given a thought to breathing. It is just a normal, continuous function of being alive.

At this time in your journey, it is necessary for you to learn to breathe deeply. The practice of inhaling deeply allows the lungs and abdomen to fully expand. Deep breathing will be very important as you move forward into the mechanics of your unfoldment process.

Technique for Deep Breathing

- ❖ Sit quietly for a few moments.
- ❖ You are going to inhale – taking a deep, deep breath to the count of seven,
- ❖ Hold to the count of seven.
- ❖ Exhale slowly to the count of seven.
- ❖ Sit quietly another minute or two.

❖ Repeat the process three times.

❖ Continue your practice of the art of breathing daily, until you are comfortable and can breathe deeply and comfortably on command.

The Art of Relaxation

What does it mean to relax? Webster defines relaxation as "…to make less tense or rigid; to relieve nervous tension or anxiety; to loosen up, to ease, to seek rest." Relaxation can be described in three words— "simply, let go!"

It is common in our society for us to be continuously involved in something. Our culture is one of action and one of doing. If we are not working, we are golfing, shopping, stopping for a cold drink or a hot cup of coffee. We go on vacation and we continue rushing here and there. We never seem to have the time to just "be." Many of us have a job which may subject us to pressures, such as schedules, travel, a disagreeable supervisor or employee, mood swings, etc. All of these factors allow us to become subjected to stress, ulcers, and high-blood pressure, along with many other diseases. Every day, there may be some sort of stress, tension, unhappiness, or a myriad of other negative issues. We can better deal with these issues by learning the practice of the art of relaxation.

It is a common practice in our society to take care of our bodies; we attempt to lose weight, we go to the gym, we ride our bicycle, we have regular physical checkups by our doctor. This is good; however, in doing these things, we are still in an action mode.

You must remember the trinity of your being—you are body, mind and spirit. Your mind and your spirit need peace, tranquility and time to be allowed to "just be." When you practice breathing exercises in your relaxation time, you are allowing your body to become oxygenated. The practice of relaxation will improve your mental capacity. It will also increase your efficiency. It will remove the pressures of the day and prevent you from the various diseases caused by stress and tension. It may not be possible for you to stop in your busy day for a fifteen minute relaxation or meditation; however, there are little things you can do during the day to release tensions and provide a degree of relaxation. You can stretch, you can take a few deep breaths, or you can just stop short and do absolutely nothing for sixty seconds. While it is important to recognize the need for exercise of your body, you must consider your mind and spirit as well. In order to do so, it is necessary that you establish a time for complete relaxation.

Technique for Relaxation

Now it is time to relax your body, mind and spirit.

Get out your journal and make sure all the prerequisites have been followed.

Enter your chamber (the place chosen for your unfoldment process). If you desire, switch on your relaxation music, choose your level of lighting, light a candle or prepare your choice of incense. Do whatever makes you feel at ease.

Sit in your comfortable chair, close your eyes and just let go.

Inhale and take a deep, deep breath to the count of seven, hold it to the count of seven, and now exhale to the count of seven, and just let go. Deep breathing prepares you for entering into a relaxed state. Breathe again, and then do it once more.

Now, Just be!

As you continue in your practice, you will realize that your mind can not relax until your body is relaxed. If you have difficulty in relaxing the body, try using the Countdown of Relaxation. This method is relaxing each area of the body, working from the toes to the top of the head.

Start the relaxation process. Begin by taking three deep breaths, feel the tension in the body dissipating.

Start the countdown. This is simply accomplished by being still and saying or thinking:

❖ I am relaxing my toes; feel the tension dissipating.
❖ I am relaxing my feet; feel the tension dissipating.
❖ I am relaxing my ankles; feel the tension dissipating.
❖ I am relaxing the calf's of my legs; feel the tension dissipating.
❖ I am relaxing my knees; feel the tension dissipating.

Continuing relaxing right on up, relaxing the thigh, the abdomen, the chest, the arms, the neck the face—right to the top of your head.

Feel the relaxation in every muscle of your body. Feel the wave of relaxation soothing your body, mind, and Spirit. When the body has become relaxed, once again take three deep breaths in to the count of seven, holding each for the count of seven, and exhaling to the count of seven. Just sit in the quiet, at peace, and just be!

Never force yourself to relax. It must come with ease. Do not be discouraged if mastering the process of relaxing seems to be slow. Continue your relaxation sessions daily. You must be consistent and persistent. You must develop an attitude of confidence and success. Every step you take each day is bringing you one step closer to your final goal. You must be fully capable of relaxing the body, mind and spirit before you move on to the next process of The Art of Concentration.

<u>*The Art of Concentration*</u>

You have mastered the ability to deep breathe and to relax. Be proud of your achievements! The next step is learning the proper method of concentration. What is concentration? In *Contemporary Definitions of Psychic Phenomena and Related Subjects* by SAM, Inc., it states

> "Concentration is the application of one's total attention to a specific; attuning the mind continuously to a focal point; one single thought. It is the ability to focus the mind upon a given point or object and hold it there to the exclusion of all else."

There are two types of concentration to be considered. They are spontaneous or automatic concentration and deliberate controlled concentration.

Spontaneous or automatic concentration:

> It is defined as "the function of the mind, under impulse or a strong interest that maintains the mind on one line of thought."

Deliberate or controlled concentration:

It is defined as "forcing the mind to think on one specific subject." The subject matter may be something of little interest to you, but required of you. An example might be a school homework assignment.

Concentration is a mental process. Controlled concentration is the type of concentration which is a necessary step in reaching your goal of using your innate abilities. What is the procedure to follow? You will be applying the previous techniques by removing all distractions from yourself externally and internally. Your chamber has been prepared to allow you the silence necessary for you to proceed. It is now important that you shut out all internal discussion. This means you must remove unwanted thoughts from your mind—shut down the mental chatter, let go of any turmoil in your life. Turn your mind away from all the cares of your mental and physical world. Basically, you are detaching your mind in order to enable it to focus on one thought, subject, or object. As you move forward in the later steps of the process you will understand why you must be able to focus, to concentrate.

Technique for the Art of Concentration

It is time to start your first session of controlled concentration. You have already mastered the art of breathing, relaxation. If an unwanted thought seeps in your concentration session, just say "out of my consciousness" and then go back to your point of concentration of the object. Every time an unrelated thought seeps in, use the same expression to detach your mind from it; and, allow yourself to go back into the state of concentration on the object. For this practice session, the object will be a long stemmed red rose.

❖ Enter your chamber.
❖ Have your journal near by.

❖ Turn the lights down low, or light a candle.

❖ Sit in a comfortable position.

❖ Choose an object (a long-stemmed red rose).

❖ Enter a relaxed state. Sit in this state a few seconds.

Now, for two or three minutes, observe every detail of the beautiful red rose from the bottom of its long stem to the beautiful flower. Focus intently on the rose. Visualize every aspect of the long green stem, the thorns, the distance between the small branches of leaves, how many leaves on each, the base upholding what once was a bud, the open rose and its petals, how the petals lap one upon the other creating the completeness of the rose. Concentrate on the size, color, depth and every little detail. Let each of the facets of the rose register very clearly in your mind.

❖ Turn away from the rose.

❖ Write in your journal every detail you can remember of the long stemmed rose (and write down all the other unrelated thoughts that seeped in)

❖ Draw a line under the last item on your list.

❖ Next, turn again to the rose and view it from the bottom of the stem, to the top of the flower and check off each item you have on your list.

❖ Add any additional items you missed during your concentration period.

❖ Make yourself a list of objects to be used in each succeeding practice session. Practice daily. Be consistent and persistent. This daily practice will soon result in less time for concentration on an object as well as having more correct responses. When you are having more correct responses in less time of concentration, you have reached your goal.

Technique in the Art of Concentration for Psychokinesis (PK)

This is a demonstration of mind-over-matter. You will be required to use the method of controlled concentration. It can be considered deliberate focusing on an object to complete an action. In this session, you are going to bend metal. For your session, you will need your journal and a dinner fork (make sure it is one you do not need in your set).

❖ Enter your chamber once again.

❖ Enter the data in your journal (date, type of session, tools, etc).

❖ Take three deep breaths.

❖ Relax and clear your mind.

❖ Take the fork in your hand. Just below the prongs, place your index finger and thumb.

❖ Concentrate intently on the metal fork bending.

❖ Move your finger and thumb back and forth very lightly. As you concentrate on bending the fork, continue to move your fingers back and forth

❖ Feel the energy field moving as you glide your fingers lightly back and forth.

❖ Concentrate on the word 'bend.'

❖ Do not attempt to force it or try to make it bend. Do not exert your energy or put pressure on the fork. The idea is achieve total, focused concentration.

As you continue this process, you will feel the fork give and finally bend. You have achieved another step in your journey. You have allowed yourself to detach your mind from all but one subject, and that was the bending of metal. Enter the date of your success in your journal.

The time allotted for concentration will be very important when you move on to the next step. It is believed in many circles of this study, that concentration can assist you in connecting to the higher planes of existence. You have now mastered the Art of Breathing, the Art of Relaxation, and the Art of Concentration. All of these processes are stepping stones in reaching your success and will assist you in unfolding your innate abilities. At this point, you are ready to move on to the Art of the Silence.

The Art of Practicing the Silence

You must realize that sitting and relaxing the body is not the same thing as sitting in the silence. Relaxing is simply being in a state of comfort or being at ease, physically and followed by relaxing mentally. It may be wise to consider a belief of the Quaker religion in regard to the silence. They believe that silence is "the fundamental care of the soul." And that is what you are attempting to do. In the silence, you are caring for your soul.

Practicing the silence is an important step toward your goal. By entering the silence, you are allowing your mind to become free. In the silence, there is an inner calm. As an added reward, you are also nurturing your capability of becoming a better listener. It is in the silence that you can hear the still small voice within. In this same silence the voice of the universe speaks.

Every day, all day long, you are hearing noise of one sort or another. Either someone is speaking to you or speaking to someone else in your presence. Car horns are beeping, train whistles are blowing, the neighbor's dog is barking, sirens pierce the airwaves or there is that same old mental chatter going on. Every disturbance possible, threatens your peace. It is quite normal to have constant mental chatter. Thoughts run through your mind about the need for doing your job well, your need to earn additional income, or you wonder if your sick child is feeling any better. If you are to survive the constant noise, no matter what it might be, you must have time for the plain and simple—total silence.

How can you learn the art of practicing the silence? It is suggested you consider beginning with a very short period of time, perhaps two to three minutes. Why such a short span of time? It is simply because in today's world you are conditioned to a life that consists of constant noise or mental chatter. Most individuals cannot sit still for two minutes without thinking of something. It may a bill they forgot to pay, or a phone call they were supposed to make or any of the many other things that enter one's consciousness. Whatever it may be, it is interference in practicing the art of silence. Your aim is to experience a naturally serene, calm and peaceful mode of being with no thought in mind, just plain and simple silence.

Technique for Practicing the Art of Silence

The time has come to start your first session of sitting in the silence. You have already mastered the art of breathing, the art of relaxation and the art of concentration. Let's begin.

- ❖ Enter your chamber.
- ❖ Turn the lights down low, or light a candle or incense.
- ❖ Sit in a comfortable position.

Start your session by taking a few deep breaths; enter into a relaxed state. Once you are relaxed in body, mind and spirit, just sit in the silence a moment. Your aim is to experience a naturally serene, calm and peaceful mode of being with no thought in mind.

Increase your session of being in the silence day-by-day as you move along in the practice, until you can sit in the silence for the time required in each step. Do not move to the next time frame until you have mastered the required minutes suggested.

- ❖ Three minutes: Strive to achieve your first goal of three minutes constituting a session. Accomplish three sessions.
- ❖ Five minutes: Strive to achieve three sessions in the silence for five minutes.
- ❖ Seven minutes: Strive to achieve three sessions in the silence for seven minutes.
- ❖ Ten minutes: Strive to achieve three sessions in the silence for ten minutes.

You may fall asleep. That is okay. Mind you, it is not necessarily easy to get to the point of sitting in the silence when you have been so accustomed to noise. However, with daily practice you will achieve your goal. Remember practicing spasmodically is a hindrance. Once again, it is called to your attention that you must be persistent and consistent.

A very important point to remember is: Don't fool yourself and Don't give up! You are not ready to move on until you accomplish sitting in the silence for ten minutes. Once you have achieved this period of time in silence, it is time to move on to the Art of Meditation.

The Art of Meditation

The next step in the process is learning the art of Meditation. In *Contemporary Definitions of Psychic Phenomena and Related Subjects* by SAM, Inc., it is stated that:

"Meditation is defined as to muse or ponder; the quieting of one's self to listen to the still small voice within."

Meditation is not to be confused with the Art of Relaxation, the Art of Concentration or the Art of Silence. The silence should not be confused with Prayer, as prayer is the uplifting of a petition or speaking to the God of your understanding. Meditation is the reverse process; it is Universe, Spirit or God, speaking to you.

The art of meditation can also be explained as the "elevating of your subconscious, attuning with the conscious, and the awakening of the inner self." Meditation is more than just sitting in the silence. It is the art of becoming able to listen to the still small voice within. If you are in the turmoil of your daily routine, you can't hear it. That is reason you first mastered the art of practicing the silence. The practice of meditation expands your inner and outer world. Experiencing this expansion helps in developing a sense of unity, a state of being at one with the universe. Ralph Waldo Trine terms it as being "In Tune with the Infinite." It leads to self-awareness as well as to the understanding and acceptance of your self.

Meditation sessions can be as short as fifteen minutes or as long as an hour, or more. You may find that your plan for a fifteen minute meditation may extend itself. Once you check the clock, you may be amazed to find the length of time expended. Or, you may be unhappy with the fact it was very short. Just remember the four keys and that with proper "Intent, Consistency, Persistence, and Patience" you will achieve the success you seek.

Meditation not only provides an avenue for hearing the message but it may also serve your physical well-being. Your body reacts in a positive manner to the opportunity of being in the silence—at peace. Meditation provides a very special calming vibration.

Techniques for Meditation

Meditation may be accomplished in a variety of ways. Four basic methods of meditation are: by visualization, guided meditation, the Rhine method, and in groups. Appendix A, provides a listing of recommended books on the subject. A brief, basic outline is given below for these practices.

Visualization

Perhaps you may find going into a meditation session is easier for you if you use the art of Visualization. To become attuned to the stillness, you may visualize a scene that brings peace to your mind. For instance, visualize the ocean, the mountains, the forest, a large flower bed, or a meandering stream. In your mind's eye, see every aspect of the subject. Perhaps you may find comfort in some soft music, in candle light or burning incense. Attune to whatever it is that places you in an atmosphere for meditation.

Guided Meditations

If you would choose this type of meditation, several tapes are available to you. After you have prepared yourself by breathing properly, relaxing, and being in the silence, you may turn on the tape recorder and follow the voice. For example, it may lead you through an open gate on to a pathway beside a rippling brook, continuing on the path until you reach a pond. There you find several benches underneath the tall shade trees. It is there that you select a place to sit and follow the voice into a meditative state. Once you have spent the allotted time in meditation, the voice will take you back to the gate that opened into the pathway, returning you to complete conscious awareness.

The Rhine Meditation

To begin a session, enter your chamber of silence. You might light a candle, put on very soft music, burn incense or simply drift into at-oneness by the countdown method once taught by Dr. J. B. Rhine at Duke University:

❖ Outstretch your hand. Look at each finger; start the countdown from thumb to pinkie:

❖ Thumb relates to the Environment. Make peace with your environment.

❖ Index finger relates to the Physical body. Relax your body.

❖ Middle finger relates to the Conscious mind. Relax your intellect.

❖ Ring finger relates to the Subconscious mind. Relax the astral.

❖ Pinkie relates to the Spirit. Receive the Spirit in the silence.

❖ To close the meditation, start the countdown in reverse starting with the pinkie and going through each finger to the thumb.

Group Meditation

In unfolding your psychic or mediumistic abilities, one of the best methods is found in group meditations. This is a gathering of like minded individuals who meet for regular scheduled sittings. It has been proven that a mutual understanding exists in a group environment. Each sitter should be interested in the advancement of other sitters. There is no place for Ego in this environment. There must be an understanding within the group that some may unfold faster than others. You question why? It just happens that way. It could be explained that every person is at a different stage of growth and every individual has acquired their own rate of vibration and progresses accordingly.

The group offers a strong support system since it tends to pool all of the energies of the sitters. This results in vibrations that are stronger and therefore, it is very effective in the unfoldment of your innate gifts. Mental mediumship or physical mediumship may be unveiled. If you have studied and practiced all the steps outlined along the way, it may enable you in becoming a group leader.

Just Simply Meditate

When you master each of the steps outlined along the way (breathing, relaxing, concentration and entering the silence), you will soon be at a point where you may simply enter your quiet chamber, sit in your chair, close your eyes, take a few deep breaths for a moment or two and go right into meditation. This is particularly important for those intending to work from a platform in an auditorium or church. Once introduced as the medium/psychic, you must be ready to step up to the podium and in an instant attune to the higher side of life and give the messages you receive to the sitter.

Now that you have mastered the art of practicing the Art of Breathing, Relaxation, Concentration, Silence and Meditation and perhaps have fully unfolded as a Medium or Psychic, there is yet another area that may be of interest to you. It is the experience of Healing and perhaps becoming a Healer.

The Art of Healing & the Healer

Healing

One of the greatest and most wonderful gift is the gift of healing. It is another source of being of service to humankind. If a person is generally drawn to being of assistance to another, they usually have this innate ability within them. Healing can occur by giving strength to another, by bringing upliftment to one who is ill, by bringing cheer, or by being an instrument for creating healing of the body, mind or spirit. While in some individuals healing is an innate ability, others must seek to find many alternative avenues to assist in the unfoldment of their capability.

How is healing defined? In simple terms, it can be said that "healing is to make sound, well or healthy again; a restoration of health or a balancing of the body energies." We are aware that when the body is in balance, there is perfect health. When there is unbalance, there is disease.

There are many healing techniques. For instance, to name just a few, there is: spiritual healing, absent healing, contact healing or laying on of hands, magnetic healing, color healing, chakra healing, crystal healing, suggestion, as well as practices such as Qigong, Reiki, and Chios energy healing (aura and chakra), etc. Today, various methods of Alternative Healing have produced positive results and it is becoming highly respected. Find what feels best to you. Locate a good knowledgeable instructor and sign up for classes.

The Healer

What is the definition of a healer?

> "A healer is one who is able to attune to universal energies enabling bringing of the vital curative forces and stimulating energies to the diseased body, mind or spirit."

The techniques used for the healing process are many. It is up to you to seek out the method that works best for you. Every one of us is unique and has a different flow of energy in our system as well as a different rate of vibration. Therefore, one technique may work well for one and not for another. Appendix A offers a list of recommended books on Healing and the Healer.

It is necessary that the healer accomplish the art of breathing for in taking deep breaths, the healer is revitalizing the body and storing healing energies. By relaxing, the healer is allowing the absorption of the healing vibrations of the universe. By meditating and occupying the silence, the healer is attuning to Spirit and the universal forces that renew your own energy field. Each of these steps provide for the healer to be able to project the vital curative energy required to accomplish a healing. You are encouraged to follow the same process of deep breathing, relaxation, concentration, the silence and meditation.

Having accomplished these preliminaries, you have prepared yourself for properly opening the flow of energy from the universal channels. Once you have learned the appropriate technique, healing energies may be distributed to meet any need. Healing covers the balancing of the physical, emotional or mental states.

Once again, group sessions are encouraged in that there is an advantage in unfolding your healing capabilities. In a group, there is a concentration of vital energies that assist in the healing processes. When you have reached the point of feeling comfortable and confident in your healing meditations, seek out others who are interested in practicing healing techniques and work together. It is very important to note that the practice of healing requires daily meditation. It is during this practice that the healer's is revitalized.

It is wise to engage in the study of the human body, its actions and reactions. While your intuition will never let you down, the study of the human body as well as methods of practice are extremely important. As a healer, you will find great satisfaction in witnessing illnesses cured and another human being entering back into the fullness of life.

In conclusion, it is recommended that you follow each step in the outline presented herein for each new development in your unfoldment. Don't be in a hurry. Take one step at a time. Be disciplined. Study, meditate and practice living in tune with the natural law. Master each step and then find the pathway that is comfortable for you. There are many varied methods from which to choose and every individual must seek their own path. No one method works for everyone. The secret is to be consistent and persistent.

X.

CONCLUSION

Allow Your Life to go with the Flow

Y ES, YOU CAN have it all! Once you have the awareness that your goal and desire is possible, you just have to step up to the plate and do whatever it takes to bring that goal or desire into reality. You do have the power within you! Remember the four keys; you can rely on them. They are very powerful tools--

Sincere Intent,
Consistency,
Persistency,
Patience.

A simple point to remember is that "the laws are universal and they are natural and they apply to everyone and everything." The laws have never been set aside to please any individual. They are constant and ever projecting their eternal nature. Your life today, is the product of how you applied these laws yesterday. Knowingly or unknowingly, you made choices that reflect in your status today. The good thing is now that you know the laws of the game of life you can "deliberately" create your tomorrows.

No matter what has taken place in your life up to this very moment, it can all change for the better in the blinking of an eye. Thoughts do create things! The choice you make is the cause and it creates the effect. Now that you know you are co-creator, it is up to you to put things in proper perspective. If you will reflect back or perhaps concentrate on one law at a time, you will be able to create a road map for your journey. Understanding of the natural law allows you to make conscious choices that will enhance your life. It will prove that living in the flow is the answer.

There is absolutely no way to escape the Natural Law. It is a fact that you make your own happiness or unhappiness, as you obey or disobey nature's physical and spiritual laws. It is very clear that while you have options before you—you must be wise in the choices you select. Once the choice is made, without a doubt, you are forced to live with its effect. The good news is you have the ability to toss out the negative effects and allow that which you choose to replace them.

Be consciously aware that the doorway to reformation is always **open** to any human soul. You are Spirit and you have the electrical awareness of dually conditioned light acting upon your senses. This factor allows you the ability to think, talk, and be inspired by the Infinite. Reformation in the physical world alleviates a lot of disharmony in life. Recall the verse, "when I became a man, I put away childish things." Since you have grown in stature and in truth and raised your vibrations to a spiritual level, you can no longer drag the baggage of childish ways around with you. You must make proper choices and act as a responsible human being.

In living the law, you will soon realize you can live in a more suitable vibration, perhaps one of least effort. This may seem easier in regard to the physical laws. You know fire burns, so you stay away from the flame. You know if you place the fine crystal at the edge of the table, it is likely that it may be knocked off, fall to the floor, and become smithereens. You know excessive speed may bring you into the traffic court and you may face a fine. So, while it may seem easier to adapt to the physical laws, as well as the man made laws of society, it becomes apparent that those laws affect you for such a very short span of time. The physical laws come into play in your life for a mere eighty or ninety years. Perhaps, it would be wise to give some sincere consideration to the spiritual laws—for life goes on—forever! With that thought active in your mind, the Spiritual Laws should flash before your screen of life. By now, it should have become very clear that you must learn and practice the Spiritual Laws now. They are long lasting—forever.

If you obey the law, you not only create a better world for yourself but you join forces with like enlightened beings in creating a better world collectively. You can live harmoniously with your fellow beings. These laws are never ending. Live by them now. Master them now! Become so adapted to them, that your life can become one of ease. When your time comes to cross the bridge into the great beyond, the door will simply swing open to an eternity of joy, peace and understanding.

Okay, let's get serious! Now that you have read the laws and the secrets that are within them, it is time to make some genuine decisions. What is it that you really want in this life and the next? What options do you have? Certainly, you want to enhance your life. Without a doubt, you would prefer to have increased power over your circumstances. Surely you want to create the best future possible. You may also desire to assist others in finding their way in life. You may want to maximize your psychic abilities. You are, at this very moment, in the position to make the choices that will give you the results you desire for your life. Go ahead, now is the time to make a decision to be positive. It's time to go with the flow. You can do it!

Mary Robinson gave us encouragement by sharing with us that

"No body can go back and start a new beginning, but anyone can start to make a new ending."

It is a known fact that your emotional and mental vibrations are creating your future as they continually flow out consciously or unconsciously by your thoughts. Sometimes, your actions speak much louder than words. Unknowingly, you may have been creating the causes which have resulted in negative effects. This, no longer has to be the case. You can change your tomorrows. Just follow the natural law!

Ralph Waldo Emerson reminds us that:

"We are all in life's great play...comedy or tragedy, and we all have the opportunity to play all of the parts."

Select the part you wish to enact in this lifetime; it is your choice! You have read the natural law outlined herein one-by-one. The many streams of the individual natural law unites along the way and blend into the oneness of being. The natural law is there for you—day in and day out. The hassles of yesterday will disappear once you start living in the flow. Each natural law of the physical stream and each natural law of the spiritual stream, meander quietly and gently along the way, turning round the bend and blending together—in the River of Life.

APPENDIX A

Recommended Reading by Subject

Recommended Books for Spiritual Growth

Title	Author
In Tune with the Infinite	Ralph Waldo Trine
Mastering your Hidden Self	Serge King
Fate Mastered, Destiny Fulfilled	W. J. Colville
The Book of James	Susy Smith
The Art of Meditation	Joel Goldsmith
The Contemplative Life	Joel Goldsmith
Meditation, Reflections and Spiritual Philosophy	Hugh G. Burroughs
Cracking the Glass Darkly	Robert Egby
How to Use the Power of Prayer	Harold Sherman
Spiritual Unfoldment #1 and #2	White Eagle

Recommended Books to Guide in Developing Your Innate Abilities

Title	Author
Your Psychic Powers and How to Develop Them	Hereward Carrington
A Guide for the Development of Mediumship	Harry Edwards
Develop your Psychic Skills	Enid Hoffman
Expand your Psychic Skills	Enid Hoffman
Mastering your Hidden Self	Serge King
The Fine Arts of Relaxation, Concentration & Meditation	Joel & Michelle Levey
How to Meditate—A Guide to Self Discovery	Lawrence LeShan
Easy Guide to Meditation	Roy E. Davis
The Medium Touch	Joey Crinita
Guide to Mediumship	E. W. Wallis
Genuine Mediumship, The Invisible Powers	Swami Bhakta Vishita

Creative Visualization	Shakti Gawain
ESP for the Millions	Susy Smith
Extrasensory Perception	Dr. J. B. Rhine
How to Meet & Work with Spirit Guides	Ted Andrews
Ring of Chairs—A Medium's Story	Janet Cyford
Sixth Sense	Stuart Wilde
Telepathy, In Search of a Lost Faculty	Eileen Barrett
The Human Aura	Dr. Walter J. Kilner
Are you Psychic	Dr. Hans Holzer
How to Read the Aura,	
Practice Psychometry, Telepathy	W. E. Butler

Recommended Books for Healing & the Healer

Title	Author
Hands of Light	Barbara Brennan
Light Emerging	Barbara Brennan
A Guide to Spiritual Healing	Harry Edwards
The Healing Intelligence	Harry Edwards
Guide to the Understanding & Practice of Spiritual Healing	Harry Edwards
Kahuna Healing	Serge King
Insights—The Healing Paths of the Radical Spiritualist	Robert Egby
The Art of Healing	Keith Sherwood
Spiritual Healing for Today	R. Barker
The Healing Hand	Sydney Weltmer
Quantam Healing	Deepak Chopra
The Healers Manual	Ted Andrews
How to Heal with Color	Ted Andrews

APPENDIX B

Bibliography

Allen, James –*As a Man Thinketh*, Family Inspirational Library, 1973

Austin, A. W., Ed. –*Teachings of Silver Birch—Wisdom from Beyond*, Spiritual Press, 1938

Awtry, Rev. Marilyn. J. –*You and A Way*, Pub., Awtry, Inc., Fourth Ed. 1977

Awtry, Rev. Marilyn J. & Paula M. Vogt –*Contemporary Definitions of Psychic Phenomena & Related Subjects*, SAM, Inc., Arlington, VA, 1980

Awtry, Rev. Marilyn J. & Paula M. Vogt –*Natural Law Governs*, SAM, Inc., VA, 1980

Barnes, Peggy J. –*Self Realization*, Stow Foundation, Undated

Barnes, Peggy, J. –*Fundamentals of Spiritualism*, Stow Foundation, Undated

Barnes Lena J. –*Questionnaire*, Stow Foundation, Undated

Brennan, Barbara A. –*Light Emerging*, Bantam Books, 1993

Brooks, Wm. D. –*Modern Physics*, Dull, Charles E. Metcalfe, H. Clark, Henry Holt & Company, 1955

Brown, Brian, Ed. –*Wisdom of the Chinese*, Garden City Pub. Company, Undated

Carnegie University –*Cognitive Psychology* Magazine, Publisher, Carnegie University, 2005

Carrington, Hereward–*Your Psychic Powers & How to Develop Them*, Dodd, Mead & Company, 1929

Carrington & Buckland –*Amazing Secrets of the Psychic World*, Parker Pub. Co. 1975

Church of the Masters –A *New Text of Spiritual Philosophy & Religion*, 1971

Chopra, Deepak –*The Seven Spiritual Laws*, Amber Allen Pub. Company, 1994

Clark, Glenn –*The Man Who Tapped the Secrets of the Universe*, Un. of Science & Philosophy, Waynesboro, VA, 1978

Colville, Wilberforce J. *–Old & New Psychology*, Occult Publishing Company, 1897

Colville, W. J. *–Ancient Mystery & Modern Revelation*, R. E. Fenno & Company, 1910

Colville, W. J. *–Law of Suggestion & Its Application*, Reprint S.A.M. Inc., 1970

Colville, W. J. *–Life & Power from Within*, Alliance Publishing Company, 1902

Colville, W. J. *–Universal Spiritualism*, R. F. Fenno & Company, New York, 1906,

Davis, A. J. *–Questions & Answers*, Stow Foundation, Undated

Davis, A. J. *–Fire Mist to Man*, NSAC, Undated

Davis, A. J. *–The Magic Staff, an Autobiography of Andrew Jackson Davis*, J.S. Brown & Company, 1859

Davis, A. J. *–Answers to Ever-Recurring Questions*, Austin Pub. Company, CA, 1926

Davis, A. J. *–The Harmonial Philosophy*, Advanced Thought Pub. Company, Old

Debray, Stanley *–Psychical Research, Science & Religion*, Methuen & Co., Old & Undated

Donne, Dr. John *–Devotion, Upon Emergent Occasions*, Thesaurus of Quotations, E. Fuller, New York

Drummond, Henry D. *–Drummond Addresses*, M.A. Donohue & Co., Chicago, Very Old

Drummond, Henry D. *– Natural Law in the Spiritual World*, Very Old,

Drummond, Henry D. *–Ascent of Man*, James Pott & Company, 1898

Durant, Will *–The Mansions of Philosophy*, Simon & Schuster, Inc., 1929

Eddington, A. S. *–Science & the Unseen* World, MacMillan Company, 1929

Emerson, Ralph Waldo *–Every Man's Library*, Ed. E. Rhy, J. M. Dent & Sons, 1906

Emerson, R. W. *–Essays 1st & 2nd Series*, Richard Clay & Sons, 1906

Emerson, R. W *–Select Essays of Emerson*, American Book Company, 1907

Findlay, Arthur *–Rock of Truth*, Psychic Press, Ltd., 1948

Fitzgerald, Dr. B. J. *–A New Text of Spiritual Philosophy & Religion*, Published by Universal Church of the Masters, 1972

Fortune, Dion *–Cosmic Doctrine*, Society Of Inner Light, 1976

Foster, E. M. *–Greek View of Life*, Ann Arbor Paperbacks, 1967

Goldsmith, Joel *–Practicing the Presence*, Harper & Row, 1961

Goldsmith, Joel *– The Infinite Way*, Willing Publishing Company, 1956

Goldsmith, Joel *– The Letters*, Published by Joel S. Goldsmith, 1949

Goldsmith, Joel *– The World is New*, Compton Printing Ltd., 1949

Goldsmith, Joel *– Thunder of Silence*, Harper & Row, 1961

Hall, Manly P. *–Questions & Answers*, Philosophical Research Society, 1946

Hicks, Jerry & Ester *–A New Beginning*, Varsity Books, Reprint 1994

Hudson, Thomas *–Law of Psychic Phenomena*, Pub. by Samuel Weiser, N.Y., 1968

Jones, Kenyon *–God's World*, Lightning Source Inc., 1919

Keeler, F. W. *–Practice of Concentration*, Lakeside Unity Temple, 1979

King, Serge *–Mastering Your Hidden Self*, Theosophical Publishing House, 1985

Lamsa, Dr. George *–And the Scrolls Opened*, Doubleday & Co., Inc. N.Y. 1967

Lodge, Sir Oliver *–Life & Matter*, J. P. Putnam & Son, 1906

Lodge, Sir Oliver *–Man & Universe*, Methuen & Co., London, 1908

Logan, Daniel *–Do You Have ESP?*, Doubleday & Company, Inc. 1970

Long, Max Freedom *– The Secret Science at Work*, DeVorss & Co., 1953

Mitchell, Edgar D. *–Psychic Explorations – A Challenge for Science*, G. P. Putnam & Sons, New York, 1974

Moses, W. Stainton (pen name M. A. Oxen) *–Spirit Teaching: The Mediumship of William Stainton Moses*, 1883

Myers, F. W. H. *–Science & a Future Life*, MacMillan & Company, 1893

Owen, Robert Dale *– The Debatable Land between This World and the Next*, London; Trubner, 1871

Rhine, J. B. *–New Frontiers of the Mind*, New York: Farrar & Rinehart, 1937

Rhine, Dr. J. B. *–Extra-Sensory Perception after Sixty Years*, Holt: New York, 1940

Rhine, L. E. *–Hidden Channels of the Mind*, William Sloane Publishing, 1961

Rosicrucian's *–Magnus Incognito, The Secret Doctrine of the Rosicrucians*, Yoga Publishing Society, 1949

Russell, Walter *–Message of the Divine Iliad*, Jarman Press, 1949

Russell, Walter *–The Secret Light*, The Walter Russell Foundation, 1947

Sabine, W. H. W. –*Second Sight in Daily Life,* Coward-McCann, Inc., N.Y. 1949

Smith, Susy –*Power of the Mind,* Chilton Book Co., 1975

Smith, Susy –*The Book of James,* G. P. Putnam & Son, 1974

Swami Bhakta Vishita –*Genuine Mediumship,* 1919

Three Initiates –*Kybalion,* Yogi Publishing Society, 1940

Tolle, Echart –*Power of Now, A Guide to Spiritual Enlightenment,* New World Library, Novato, California, 1999

Trine, Ralph Waldo –*In Tune with the Infinite,* Dodge Publishing Company, l897

Trine, R.W. –*Character Building & Thought Powers,* Thomas Y. Crowell & Co., 1900

Trine, R.W. –The *Higher Powers of the Mind & Spirit,* Dodge Publishing Company, 1917

Trobridge –George, *Swedenborg, Life & Teaching,* Swedenborg Foundation, 1949

Tuttle, Hudson –*Mediumship & Its Laws,* Reprint by NSAC

White, Steward –*Unobstructed Universe,* E. P. Dalton, 1940

Wilde, Stuart –*Sixth Sense,* Hay House Inc., 2000

Urantia –*The Urantia Book,* Urantia Foundation, 1955

White Eagle –*Spiritual Unfoldment #1,* White Eagle Publishing Company, England, l982

White Eagle –*Wisdom from White Eagle,* White Eagle Publishing Company, England, l967

White Eagle –*The Quiet Mind,* White Eagle Publishing Company, England, l979

Wolfe, N. B. –*Startling Facts about Spiritualism,* N. B. Wolfe, l 874

Zukav, Gary –*The Seat of the Soul,* Simon & Schuster, l989

Note: SAM, INC was incorporated my Marilyn J. Awtry and Paula Vogt. It stands for 'Spiritualism and More."

APPENDIX C

Reference Material

American Heritage College Dictionary – 3rd Edition, Houghton Mifflin Company, 1997

Chinese Analects –6th Century, Undated

Edwards, T. – *The New Dictionary of Thought,* Compiled by Tryan, Standard Bk. Co., 1984

Henry, Lewis C. – *Five Thousand Quotations for all Occasions,* Double Day, 1945

Kipfer, Barbara A., PhD, Ed. –*Roget's 20th Century Thesaurus*, Dell Pub. Co., N.Y., 1992

Kipfer, B.A., Ph.D, Ed. – *Roget's 21ˢᵗ Century Thesaurus*, Dell Pub. Co., NY, 1992

The Holy Bible – Revised NKJV, *Book of Luke,* and *Book of Matthew*

The Holy Bible – KJV, *Book of Philippians* and *Book of John*

Webster, Merriam – *Webster Collegiate Dictionary,* Tenth Edition, 1998

Quotes

Bartlett, John –*Familiar Quotations*, 13th Ed., Little, Brown & Co, Boston & Toronto, 1955

Bartlett, John – *Familiar Quotations*, 10th Edition, Blue Ribbon Books, NYC, 1919

Braude, Jacob M., Compiled and Edited — *Braude's Second Encyclopedia of Stories, Quotations & Anecdotes*, Prentice Hall, N.J., 1957

Braude, Jacob M. *–The Speaker's Desk Book of Quips, Quotes, &* *Anecdotes,*Prentice Hall, N.J., 1963

Edwards, Tryan, D.D. –Compiler, *The New Dictionary of Thought*, Std. Book Co., 1955

Halycon House *–Forty Thousand Quotations*, Pub. Halcyon House, 1937

Henry, Lewis C. *–Five Thousand Quotations for all Occasions*, Double Day & Co., New York, 1945

Zig Ziglar *–Quotable Quotes*, Gramacy Books, 1999

ABOUT THE AUTHOR

 Marilyn J. Awtry has become known as the Walking Encyclopedia of Spiritualism of the 20th Century having been a researcher in the field of Spiritualism for over forty-five years. She is well-known as an orator, teacher, and author having 30 publications to her credit. She is the USA Correspondent for the English newspaper entitled the Psychic World as well as columnist for The National Spiritualist Summit. She has been a featured columnist in several secular and spiritual magazines.

For three years, Marilyn served as Editor of Speakout, a monthly publication of The Harmonial Philosophy Association. She also was owner and Editor of a monthly paper The Cassadagan.

She has been listed in Who's Who of American Women, Who's Who of Women of the World and Cambridge Who's Who 2010-11 Edition. The National Geographic Traveler's Magazine featured a full-page article about her varied endeavors. Marilyn was featured on the Maury Povich TV Show—a story about the Southern Cassadaga Spiritualist Association in Florida.

Her latest endeavor is the founding of her own publishing company, Shen-men Publishing located in Sanford, Florida.

CPSIA information can be obtained at www.ICGtesting.com
Printed in the USA
LVOW07s2159080215

425990LV00001B/3/P

9 780983 064107